LIZ CURTIS HIGGS
AN ENCOURAGER®

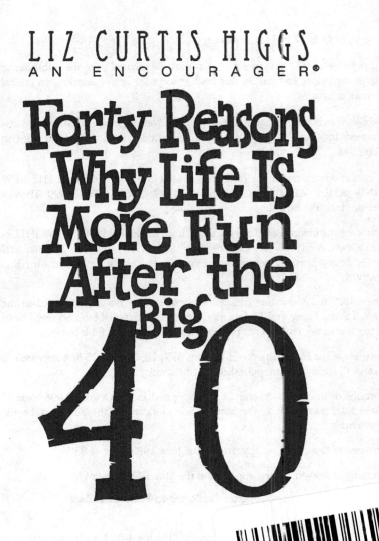

Forty Reasons Why Life Is More Fun After the Big 40

A
JANET
THOMA
BOOK

THOMAS NELSON PUBLISHERS
Nashville • Atlanta • London • Vancouver

Published in Nashville, Tennessee, by Thomas Nelson, Inc., Publishers, and distributed in Canada by Word Communications, Ltd., Richmond, British Columbia.

Unless otherwise noted, the Bible version used in this publication is THE NEW KING JAMES VERSION. Copyright © 1979, 1980, 1982, 1990 Thomas Nelson, Inc., Publishers.

Scripture quotations noted NIV are taken from the HOLY BIBLE, NEW INTERNATIONAL VERSION ®. Copyright © 1973, 1978, 1984 by International Bible Society. Used by permission of Zondervan Publishing House. All rights reserved.

The "NIV" and "New International Version" trademarks are registered in the United States Patent and Trademark Office by International Bible Society. Use of either trademark requires the permission of International Bible Society.

Portions of the Introduction and Reasons 5, 7, 18, 19, and 25 first appeared in *Today's Christian Woman*, published by Christianity Today, Inc.

Portions of Reasons 3, 5, and 14 first appeared in the October 1996 issue of *Home Life*, published by the Sunday School Board of the Southern Baptist Convention.

Portions of Reason 9 first appeared in the June 1993 issue of *BBW*.

Portions of Reason 28 first appeared in the May 1996 issue of *Home Life*.

Library of Congress Cataloging-in-Publication Data

Higgs, Liz Curtis.
    Forty reasons why life is more fun after the big 4-0 / Liz Curtis Higgs.
        p. cm.
    ISBN 0-7852-7615-7 (pbk.)
    1. Middle age—Humor.   I. Title.
PN6231.M47H54   1997
818'.5402—dc20

Printed in the United States of America.

1 2 3 4 5 6 — 02 01 00 99 98 97

Dedication

This book is dedicated with joy and abandon to my sweet husband, Bill, who proved to me that life really could be fun after 40, two years before I discovered it for myself. Beloved, you are both the wind beneath my wings and the foot behind my desk chair. Thank you for making me write until it's right. I love you, Bill!

Other Books by Liz Curtis Higgs:

For Women:

"One Size Fits All" and Other Fables
Only Angels Can Wing It, the Rest of Us Have to Practice
Reflecting His Image

For Children:

The Pumpkin Patch Parable
The Parable of the Lily
The Sunflower Parable

Contents

Acknowledgments

This book would be very slim indeed without the comments and stories submitted by more than four hundred women from more than forty states, plus Canada, Germany, and Australia. Your honesty, genuineness, and sense of humor came through on each survey. Bless you!

Hugs also go to Heather Fields, who carefully entered all those surveys and stories onto a computer disk, making my life (and my summer!) so much easier.

Special thanks to my editorial sisters at *Today's Christian Woman*, Ramona Cramer Tucker and Jane Johnson Struck, who saw the potential in three little paragraphs about turning 40 and suggested we expand them into an article, which turned into a book. Bless you for being two of my favorite encouragers!

To my friends, old and new, at Thomas Nelson books, especially my editorial team, Janet Thoma and Todd Ross, thank you for being such pros.

Texas-size kudos to Dennis Hill, artistic genius, whose clever illustrations inhabit this book and make it come alive visually. You are a blessing, brother!

Hugs and kisses to my two "tea" sisters, Sara Fortenberry and Lonnie Hull DuPont, whose constant encouragement keeps me on track.

Finally, forty candles for each reader who invests in the health of her funny bone by buying my books and sharing them with friends. You are the reason I do what I do. I can never thank you enough for inviting me into your life!

"*Forty* Reasons"?
I can't even think of three.

The day I turned 40 dawned like any other summer Sunday morning: It was hot and I was bothered. I slapped off the alarm clock, whining to no one in particular, "Help! I'm 40 and I can't get up."

My children offered zero comfort. Ages 5 and 7 at the time, they were too young to buy me presents and too old not to notice my advancing age (prompted by their father, of course). "Happy Birthday, Mom!" they sang out as I trudged down the steps. "Gee, you do look older!"

The morning went downhill from there. At church, it was lots of good-natured ribbing in the vestibule after the service. Oh sure, ha-ha-ha, over the hill, thank you very much. By two o'clock it was depression city, thanks to a silent phone, an empty mailbox (even if it was Sunday), and the absence of gifts from my husband ("Gosh, honey, you said you didn't need anything!").

The only party at my house was a pity party. The only card I got said, "Once you hit 40, you gotta be careful . . . At your age, it's hard to get new parts."

Harrumph. I crawled off to bed for a midafternoon nap, hoping I'd wake up a happier woman—or 30 again.

When I opened my eyes an hour later, I was still a decade older but well rested enough to face the truth: The Big 4-0 had arrived, and there was nothing I could do but accept it. Yes, even celebrate it.

I took a deep breath, leaped out of bed, and headed for the family room. "I'm up!" I called out. And finally, I was.

For the next forty chapters, I am heaven-bent to help *you* up and out of the doldrums of approaching midlife. We'll laugh about some of the weird stuff that shows up when you turn 40—chin hair, gray hair, no hair. We'll eavesdrop on more than four hundred women (and some exceptional men) who have faced 40 and lived to share their spin on things. You'll see their names and ages here—women from all over the country who hula-hooped through the fifties, twist-and-shouted through the sixties, *Working Woman*ed through the seventies, shopped through the eighties, and downsized in the nineties. They're an experienced bunch.

At the end of every other chapter, you'll read a story of a unique 40th birthday celebration. Some are funny, some are outrageous, others are clever ideas for the birthday women on *your* future party list. (If you try the one with the duct tape and the office chair, please don't tell people you read about it here!)

Certain themes popped up again and again, like these helpful words of advice from Carol who warned, "Everyone says life begins at 40. Sure . . . it begins falling apart!" She's right, but she's not telling you the whole story.

Turning 40 boils down to good news and bad news.

Bad news? Skin tags. Facial hair. Varicose veins. You always wanted to grow up to be like your mom, right? You made it!

Good news? No more agonizing over what it will be like to turn 40. You did it ("Whew!") and you survived.

More good news? Wisdom. It only comes with age. You can't buy it, rent it, or surf your way to it on the Internet. Wisdom comes, not from always doing things right, but from living through doing things *wrong* and learning something in the process. I'm not all the way to wise yet, but I'm en route. So are you. Linda, 51, assures us, "Forty is the beginning of real adulthood. All the things you start losing (like the ability to travel without an eighteen-inch magnifying mirror) are more than made up for with the first tiny inklings of wisdom."

Personally, I hurry past most mirrors, especially magnifying ones, but I get the point: What time taketh away, the Lord giveth back in wisdom. Shawn, 49, insists, "I wouldn't trade my life or my age with anyone. Sometimes I wish I had the energy and pep of my younger years but the experiences and wisdom of growing and maturing are worth more." Let's be honest. Wisdom isn't what most of us are obsessing over. We're thinking about how many days we can go between wax jobs—and I'm not talking about the car. We're worrying about developing a permanent squint from trying to read distant road signs or small-print Bibles or bedside alarm clocks. Or the big E on the eye exam chart.

I asked my friend Rosi, "When are you turning 40?"

Her reply was solemn and specific: "One hundred thirty-nine days."

This birthday is a big countdown. Caren, 42, said, "Before I hit 40, I thought it was just a number in your head. Now I know it's also in your back, shoulders, knees, and feet." She forgot to mention your elbow, a body part you hardly ever think about unless you bang it on a table (Ouch! Right on the funny bone!). It was precisely that not-so-funny bone that sent me to an orthopedist for the first time.

"Tennis elbow," the doctor assured me, as he filled a hypodermic needle with cortisone.

I laughed out loud. "Tennis? I haven't played tennis since I was 18!"

"Liz, that's what this injury is *called*, not what causes it," he responded with a patient sigh. "You'll feel a little pressure now."

They used those exact words nine years ago when I was about to give birth to an almost twelve-pound baby, so I hung on to the examination table for dear life. When it turned out to be just that—a little pressure—I exhaled with relief and asked, "If this pain isn't caused by tennis, then what *has* happened?"

"You don't really want to hear it."

"It's *my* elbow. Of course I want to hear it."

Now that I've heard it, I never want to hear it again.

Trouble is, I *keep* hearing it from the lips of every professional person I've visited ever since: "Well, now that you're over 40 . . ."

My optometrist said it when she intoned that dreaded word, *bifocals*.

My dentist said it when she gently pointed out my "receding gum line."

My internist said it when she discussed the concept of "zero metabolism."

My gynecologist said it when she whispered ominously, "premenopausal."

My hairstylist said it when she tried to fluff hair that's no longer there due to "hormonal hair loss."

My cosmetician said it while she plucked and clucked over "hormonal hair *gain*."

Laurie, 49, sums it up perfectly: "Being over 40 means the products you bought with a lifetime guarantee begin to wear out." Or as Sue, 47, puts it, "Like an aging car, your body, little by little, one thing at a time, begins to go and just doesn't work like it used to."

Starting with elbows.

When I told people I was writing a book called *Forty Reasons Why Life Is More Fun After the Big 4-0*, those already over 40 looked at me as if I'd grown a third ear. "*Forty* reasons? Boy, you've got your work cut out for you there." Younger women like Sue Ann, 32, tried to be helpful but reported, "I took a survey in the office of those who are over 40, and none of them could think of anything good or amusing."

I'm not discouraged. I'm a woman who insists the glass is half *full*. As my friend Kathy once told me, "Liz, I have this picture of meeting you in heaven as the director of an awesome and holy jug band with a *very* strong kazoo section!" Some of us just prefer to focus on the positive side of life and skip the rest. The bad stuff will show up anyway—why organize a welcoming committee?

As a junior student of the Scriptures, I'm curious about one thing: Why is the number forty such a hot item in the Bible?

You've got your basic forty days and forty nights of rain with Noah, forty days on Mount Sinai for Moses, forty days of fasting in the desert for Jesus, and the forty days the risen Lord spent walking around Jerusalem affirming His resurrection.

Furthermore, Isaac was 40 when he married Rebekah, Esau was 40 when he married Judith, and the Israelites wandered in the desert eating manna for forty years. (Forty years of one food? Pizza might work for my kids, but forty years of something translated as "what is it?"? Not at my house.) Forty was also a favorite with kings: David ruled for forty years, as did Solomon and a guy named Joash. So, what's the big biblical deal about forty?

For the definitive answer, I turned to my hubby, Bill, the one with the Ph.D. in Hebrew (long story). He explained that forty is a very significant number—an entire generation. It's also the age at which a person was considered "full grown." (Good, because this is as full grown as I want to get.) Forty was how long critical situations lasted—testings, trials (that flood thing again), and judgment. In those days, if you made it through to 41, the light from the promised land was on the horizon. Unless you're Moses, in which case the glow was a burning bush. For the rest of us, it's the blaze from the candles on our birthday cakes, setting off smoke alarms.

Karri, 39, thinks just getting to 40 is "impressive!" Let's face it. Many of our acquaintances never made it this far. I hate to bring up such a morbid truth, but one of the (unstated) reasons why life is more fun after 40 is because you're *alive* to celebrate it. An attitude of gratitude, that's the life for me.

For many of us, 40 is when our creative expression takes wing. Artists, speakers, and authors often don't touch canvas, microphone, or word processor until they've accumulated enough "been there" maturity to have something to paint, say, or write. Absolutely no disrespect meant, but few audiences would pay to hear the musings of a 20 year old. We want to hear from a woman who has traveled down the road far enough to have taken a few rocks in her Reeboks.

As for the stories I'll be sharing in this book, I agree with Jack, 47, who wrote at the top of his book survey, "This is all original, and mostly true." Couldn't have summed it up better myself!

My daughter, Lillian, then 7, asked me at lunch one day, "Why do adults only read a book once?"

"Well, after you know how the story ends, it's not as fun to read it a second time," I explained, then hastened to add, "But if it's really well written, it's worth reading again; the first time for the story, the second time to savor the literary skills of the writer."

My 9-year-old son, Matthew, nodded emphatically. "I know just what you mean, Mom. I've read *Donkey Kong Country* three times!"

Hmmm.

I'm not sure you'll need to read *Forty Reasons* again and again in order to savor my so-so skills as a wordsmith. But whenever you need a lighthearted reminder that life after 40 is survivable, even enjoyable—I'm here for you, girlfriend!

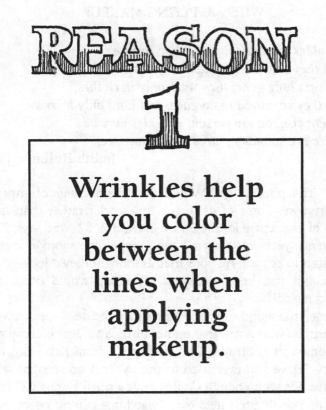

REASON

1

Wrinkles help
you color
between the
lines when
applying
makeup.

WRINKLES HELP YOU COLOR BETWEEN THE LINES WHEN APPLYING MAKEUP.

Wrinkles are one thing I've had to face,
And they seem to turn up every place.
In years long gone, they were only in clothes,
But they've moved to my face, and Lord only knows
Where else, on my person, wrinkles may be . . .
There are so many places that I can't see!

                                    Judith Huffman, 51

This poet is right: Wrinkles are the first sign of impending Fortydom. Some of us "crack up" sooner rather than later. Others of us prepare for the future like Carol, 52, who says, "The last twenty years of using all those expensive wrinkle creams really start to pay off. All your friends thought they'd look young forever, but you knew a day of reckoning would occur and planned ahead!"

Women the world over face wrinkles, like Sue, 41, from western Australia who noted that on her birthday, "Over half my gifts were some sort of cream!" Or Beverley, 41, from Kentucky, who mourns, "Have you ever tried to put eyeliner on straight when you have lids with enough skin to graft a small elephant?" Patty, 40, from Washington, frets over "watching a hundred or more age spots cover your skin . . . How many gallons of age spot cream will I use in the next twenty years?"

Maybe instead of those teensy little half-ounce containers, they could package wrinkle-and-spot creams in giant econo-size tubs like margarine. Of course they'd cost $7,439.26 but think of the savings in time and trips to the beauty counter!

Soon after my 40th (how *did* they know?), I received an envelope in the mail filled with slick literature about a wrinkle-minimizing system. Not just a cream, not merely a moisturizer, this was all that and more: a *pill*. A pill "based on the work of a famed Scandinavian skin specialist" (who wasn't putting his/her name on *anything*). It was advertised as a "quantum leap in the war on wrinkles . . . works from the inside out!"

Well, I *am* working on my wrinkles from the inside out. My goal is to stay plump enough to keep those wrinkles nicely filled up and therefore save $154.85 on a three-month supply of their wrinkle-minimizing system. If you're going to spend $1.72 a day, why not just buy three jelly donuts? It would accomplish the same thing and be more fun.

Mikki, 54, tracked down something called "Turnaround Cream." She wrote, "It's supposed to reverse the aging process. Now I have the skin of a teenager. All I need to know is, do they still make Clearasil?"

My friend and favorite funny lady, Jeanne Robertson, 53, has been speaking and traveling the country for thirty years. As Jeanne puts it, "At this point, I lie in the bed at night and hear myself wrinkling. It wakes me up. The wrinkling comes in loud and clear because it is happening so near my ears. One night my husband sat right up in the bed and whispered, 'The house is settling . . . or is that you wrinkling again?'"

No doubt about it, our families are the first to offer encouragement when it comes to wrinkles. Merrigay was assured by her 12-year-old daughter, "Mom, you don't have wrinkles, the fat on your face is just squishing together!" Cindy, 47, had it all explained to her by her 14-year-old daughter:

> *When I turned 40, she tried some of my new astringent, only to complain that it made her face sting. When I said it didn't make mine sting, she reasoned, "Well, that's probably because your skin's more developed."*
>
> *"More developed? What do you mean?" I asked.*
>
> *She sweetly explained, "You know, it's just been there longer."*

Children are fascinated by wrinkles. Beverly, 58, from Colorado admits, "My little granddaughter, age 4, wonders why I have so many cracks in my face."

Our son, Matthew, tries to count the rings in my neck to determine my age, like an ancient sequoia. Daughter Lillian likes to fit her little finger in the grooves so she can, in her words, "drive all over my face." Lovely.

Speaking of driving, let's climb into the car with Virginia from Oklahoma:

> *Our family was traveling down the highway for a weekend outing and I was working on a stitchery project in the front seat. As I was busily stitching, I got this feeling that someone was staring at me and looked up to find my daughter Betty, 9, leaning over the backseat carefully examining my face. With all the innocence in the world she sweetly proclaimed, "Mommy, did you know that your Oil of Olay isn't working?!"*
>
> Virginia, 54

"Mommy, did you know that your Oil of Olay isn't working?"

Or as Maxine, 47, says, "Oil of Delay is my best friend!"

On those rare occasions when I invest in a facial, I have to put up with sound effects hovering above my face: "Oh dear, my, my, tsk, tsk, hmm, hmm." Bobbe, 40, knows just what I'm talking about with "this version of adult acne where the skin doesn't 'slough' off like it used to and you end up with clogged pores due to poor sloughing . . . doesn't that beat all?"

Good news: Once those pesky blemishes are gone, you can use concealer all over your face. Just don't make the same mistake I do of confusing the flesh-colored tube of concealer with my almost identical tube of anti-feathering lipstick base. I end up with blemishes that don't feather and lips you can't see!

I long for the days when I could face the world *sans* makeup, when moisturizer was something you smoothed on your legs after a day in the sun, when Noxema and water kept you looking dewy fresh around the clock, when your face didn't look as though you slept in it. Pat, 58, agrees: "Every year it takes more moisturizer and 'paint' in order to look good. It's hard to find room to pack all my skin-care products when we go on vacation. My husband says he'll have to rent a U-haul if my maintenance kit gets much larger."

The Good News Is . . .

Wrinkles not only come from time and the sun, they also come from laughing at the absurdities of life, which increase exponentially after 40. They also come from looking surprised when your child hands you a woolly worm from the garden. They come from smiling when you see an old friend who is as wrinkled as you are. They are a road map of experiences that you alone have enjoyed.

I'm learning to embrace the psalmist's words, "The lines have fallen to me in pleasant places."[1] Even if they have fallen on my face, at least I can keep track of them there, knowing every single wrinkle was earned with time well spent.

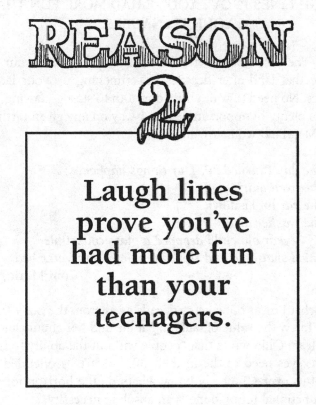

REASON
2

Laugh lines
prove you've
had more fun
than your
teenagers.

LAUGH LINES PROVE YOU'VE HAD MORE FUN THAN YOUR TEENAGERS.

The best kind of wrinkles are the ones around your eyes and lips that land after decades of scrunching up your face in hysterics. No need to wait until your 40th to start guffawing. Life will toss plenty of opportunities your way on any given birthday, as this Maryland woman will attest:

> *The day I turned 30, four things happened:*
> 1. *The oven quit.*
> 2. *The car broke down.*
> 3. *The washer died.*
> 4. *My 3-year-old child dropped a glass collectible,*
>   *which shattered and ripped a hole in our water bed.*
> **Toni Marie, 31**

See what I mean? She was a decade away from the Big 4-0, but already knew the value of laughing at life and her circumstances. Dauna from Ohio wrote that "people without the ability to laugh at themselves need to die in their 30s." Don't be offended . . . those of us over 40 merely know what's on the horizon for you, and a functional funny bone is an absolute necessity.

Ever heard the story about Sarah, the wife of Abraham? She lightened up in a hurry when God announced to her husband that she would bear a son. After all, the woman was 90! "Therefore Sarah laughed within herself, saying, 'After I have grown old, shall I have pleasure, my lord being old also?'"[2]

I asked my Bill, the Hebrew scholar of the family, just what Sarah meant when she said, "Will I have pleasure?" Somehow I didn't think she meant the pleasure of childbearing, but rather the pleasure of child-*making*. Bill's research confirmed that I was on the right track. You must admit that intimacy after 40—in this case *way* after 40—does lend itself to some entertaining moments. (See Reason 7 for more on this one!)

While we're on the subject of my dear husband, this incredibly intelligent man sometimes sports the robes of the absent-minded professor, with amusing results. One Sunday morning we were sitting side by side in church, dressed in our Sunday best, when I happened to glance down at his shoes. Correction: his *sneakers*! With his good, gray dress suit.

A flush came up my neck and around my ears. "Bill!" I whispered, fearing the worst. "Did the baby throw up on your good shoes?"

"No," he whispered back, looking confused. "Is she sick?"

"No!" I hissed. "Where are your leather wing tips?"

He looked down, then at me. "It's worse than you think. Look at my socks."

Oh no. One medium gray, one dark blue. It doesn't pay to see such things during the silent communion meditation. I closed my eyes and tried to think of important things, spiritual things, actually *anything* but my husband's feet. I'd decided never to let him dress himself again when I heard a sneeze in progress.

Out of the corner of my eye, I watched as Bill reached in his back pocket for his handkerchief and pulled out a *long* sheet of white cotton fabric, trimmed at the bottom with pinking shears and stamped with the word *Curity*—Lillian's diaper!

Good news: It was fresh from the dryer and therefore clean.

Bad news: I had to sing a solo less than two minutes after this discovery. This meant only one side of the church ever saw my face, since I couldn't risk catching an eyeful of grimy sneakers, mismatched socks, a diaper-size hankie, or my hubby's absent-minded grin.

Finding fun where you least expect it—that's life after 40, all right. Ron, a minister, was having a quiet birthday dinner with friends at a local restaurant when he received a call from the neighborhood funeral director, telling him of the death of a church member. "He wanted me to come down to the funeral home ASAP. When I arrived, he asked me to view the body first. As I approached the casket, 'the body' sat up with a camera and shouted 'Happy Birthday!' as a huge crowd appeared!"

The Good News Is . . .

Laughter is easier after 40. Your face knows the way, and you have the laugh lines to prove it. Sure, some worry lines are probably mixed in, but when you smile they can't fight the majority rule.

If you're going to turn 40 (and we hope you have or will), don't let the little stuff get you down. As my friend Ray Perez loves to point out, *birth* is big stuff, *death* is big stuff, and everything else is *little stuff*. Here's a promise for the days when you're crushed with stress, hassles, or little stuff that insists it's big stuff: "Blessed are you who weep now, / For you shall laugh."[3]

My husband and I were hosting a Sunday school class party at our home that evening. I was so busy in the kitchen warming food and bread, I didn't even notice people walking right past the kitchen door with gifts, balloons, and even a huge cake box. So I felt really clueless when I walked into the den to the yelling of "Surprise!" and there was a table filled with gifts. Of course I was showered with every mean mug and T-shirt imaginable and a black "over-the-hill" cake. The worst was yet to come. I had finally fixed a plate and sat down to eat when this man in a trench coat and a horrible ugly, old-looking mask came hobbling through the front door with a cane, hollering, "Where's my older sister?" When he sat in my lap, I was both laughing and crying. Turning 40 was definitely memorable. I am leaving town when I turn 50.

Connie from Texas, 41

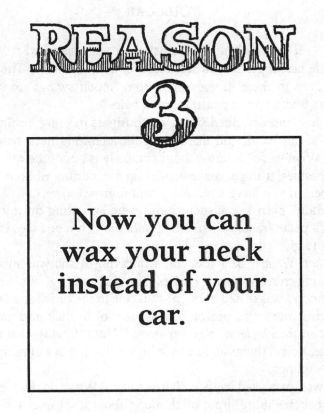

REASON 3

Now you can wax your neck instead of your car.

NOW YOU CAN WAX YOUR NECK INSTEAD OF YOUR CAR.

If you look up "neck hairs" in your standard women's midlife health guide, you will discover an awful truth: The term isn't even in there. It goes right from "mood swings" to "night sweats," with nary a pause at "neck hairs."

One friend described sitting at a business meeting, resting her chin in her hand, and discovering an inch-long neck hair . . . ugh! What to do? Yanking it out manually is out of the question, and besides, it might make it twirl up like curling ribbon. What happens if you leave it alone . . . will it grow forever?

I didn't even know such things were sprouting on my neck until a petite friend was standing under my chin one day, looked up, and giggled.

What! What is it? I thought, wondering if she was mentally counting chins or tracing creases. She said nothing, but the next afternoon I was seated in bright sunshine in the car, flipped down the visor mirror to put on a fresh coat of lipstick and gasped: *What are those?!* Neck hairs had arrived. Not soft, wispy hairs, but coarse, horrid things all in a little bunch like a grove of reforested pine saplings.

I was paralyzed with embarrassment. What do women do about such a thing? I put off thinking about it for weeks, hoping they'd fall out like the ones on the top of my head do with alarming regularity. No such luck.

This is not something you casually call up a friend to discuss. "Hey, I noticed a clump of hair on my neck today and was curious if *you* have had that experience." No way. It's just you and the friendly corner drugstore on this one. Make that the impersonal drug superstore where you can slip in and out without anyone noticing or caring about your purchase.

But of course they *do* notice, because none of the signs overhead say, "Neck Hair Solutions, Aisle Seven." So you have to ask.
I chose a woman easily a decade older than me, knowing she'd
understand. When I walked up, clearing my throat, she took one
look and said, "Aisle Two, bottom shelf."

Was it *that* obvious?

There it was, next to the "Neet" and "Nair" lotions we used as
teenagers when we wanted silky smooth legs. The "Neet for
Necks" stuff is a more potent cream that comes with a scraper
that's shaped exactly like your neck.

The Neet people obviously get it. In fact, just knowing that
this was a commercially available product had me sighing in
relief. Since my eyebrows can't handle the wax routine, I didn't
dare wax an area as sensitive as my neck (or, more accurately,
chins 2 and 3). This cream was my only hope.

I glided to the register and soundlessly slipped the package
onto the counter. The same woman stepped up. "Oh, I see you
found it!" she sang out, reaching for the cash register keys. Then
she paused, examining the box. "You don't happen to remember
the price on this stuff, do you?"

"Uh, no. I think probably . . ."

She was already on the storewide address system. "Price
check!" she hollered. "I need a price on hair remover cream. The
two-ounce cream. That's Neet . . . *N-E-E-T.* Hair remover cream.
Two ounces."

I was now a puddle on the drugstore floor. I would happily
have paid ten dollars for the stuff if we could have avoided this
little scene. Moments later, a teenager with a face full of bumps
and a mouth full of chewing gum came back on the PA, "Is that
regular or fresh scent?" He cut it off just before a blast of laughter exploded from his mouth, taking the gum with it.

"Fresh Scent," the clerk shouted back.

"Nair or Neet?"

"Neet. *N-E-E-T.* The hair remover cream, Steve. You know.
Aisle Two."

"I got it. $3.99."

I handed over the money, not making eye contact with anyone within fifty feet. Of course, there were lots of people in line behind me by this point, but I acknowledged none of them. (Probably six friends from church were back there, at least.)

"Do you want a bag for this, honey?" she asked.

"No!" I barked, then lowered my voice. "I'll just stuff it in my purse, thank you very much." I drove home quickly, avoiding my reflection in the rearview mirror.

Then, in the privacy of my old-fashioned bathroom, I courageously faced the mirror and took a deep breath. It looked easy enough. Spread evenly. Wait ten minutes or so. Remove.

I waited nervously, envisioning rashes, heart palpitations, fevers, or some other heretofore unknown reaction. Suddenly, the ten minutes were up. I guided the neck-shaped scraper all the way up to my chin and held up a hand mirror for inspection.

The beasties were gone! No nasty rash, no pain, no itch, nothing. Good grief. If I'd known it was going to be this easy, I'd have done it at the first sighting.

So, now you know. Your mother, your sister, your best friend might not tell you, but Lizzie will. Don't sweat it. And remember: $3.99 plus tax. Correct change will get you out of there *fast*.

The Good News Is . . .

Neck hairs have been around for centuries and no one has died from them.

In fact, when the beloved bridegroom in Song of Solomon praises the beauty of his bride the Shulamite, he tells her that her lips are like a strand of scarlet, her eyes are like those of a dove, and her hair resembles a flock of goats (oh, how flattering!), but *then* he says, "Your neck is like the tower of David, / Built for an armory, / On which hang a thousand bucklers, / All shields of mighty men."[4]

Now you have your answer: If anyone ever glances under your chin and says, "What are those?" you can tell them with all sincerity, "Bucklers!"

Let them figure it out.

REASON 4

Thinning hair
means you'll
use less
shampoo.

THINNING HAIR MEANS YOU'LL USE LESS SHAMPOO.

Two thousand years ago, the apostle Paul declared that "not a hair will fall from the head of any of you."[5] That may be true for those faithful few, but for the less lucky among us, it's curtains for our curly locks.

I'm not sure when the first hair slithered out of my scalp, quietly and without fanfare, but, like Hansel and Gretel, that first silken strand left behind a faint trail of shampoo crumbs for others to follow. Soon I discovered that in certain overhead lighting situations—no, it's not possible!—I could see my scalp peeking through my bottle-blonde tresses.

I marched into the hair salon, breathing threats. "What is happening to my hair?" I demanded to know. The stylists looked at one another with sorrowful expressions that translated as: *We knew this day was coming.*

I suspected that decades of bleaching, perming, hot curling, and steam rollering had taken their toll. "Is that the problem?" They shook their heads solemnly: *No, Liz.*

Wait! Maybe it's that thing Carol does with aluminum foil, white paste, and silver flaps sticking out willy-nilly all over my head. When two or three of us are gathered under a row of heat lamps, the salon looks like a *Star Trek* set. "Is *that* what's making my hair fall out, that 'going to the moon' deal?" I asked.

Again, perfectly coifed heads shook slowly back and forth: *Nooo, Liz.*

The answer is becoming more painfully clear every day, as clear as the space between Hair 372 and Hair 373 in the upper right quadrant: I am losing my hair because I am over 40 and because my mother did, too. *Oh, Mom!*

Now every morning, the looking glass is starting to make faces at me, taunting me like a recalcitrant third grader at recess:

Thinning hair! Thinning hair!
I can see your scalp is bare.
Hair was there, now it's not.
Better count the hairs you've got!

As Phyllis Diller says, "Mirror, mirror on the wall . . . I don't want to hear it."

I remember the days—this is really hard to believe—when I had to have my hair *thinned*. Betty, the owner of Betty's Beauty Parlor on Front Street, took a nasty-looking combing device filled with teensy razor blades and dragged it all through my dishwater blonde hair to thin it out. In theory this was supposed to make my pageboy look smoother.

Memo to Betty: If you saved my hair in a dustpan somewhere, please send it back.

When men start getting a little light on top, it's a big joke. Ha-ha, male pattern baldness, nah-nah, it's your turn—that kind of thing. Most of my sweet Bill's hair left town before we even married, and I have the wedding pictures to prove it. Being the sensitive wife that I (sometimes) am, I must suppress the occasional desire to blurt out, "Look at all the thick, wavy hair that man over there has!" Or worse, stare at Bill's scalp and murmur, "I wish those stray hairs on top would just fall off, so you could be *really* bald like Jean-Luc Picard." Instead, I kiss his smooth head often and whisper words of encouragement about how his brainy cranium simply pushed out all the hair follicles.

What are Mr. Bill and Ms. Liz to do? Try that expensive hair growth stuff in the infamous pink and blue boxes? I don't think so. Ever read the fine print? Every day, forever. Big bucks a month, every month, forever. Rub into your scalp twice a day, forever. Reality check: It ain't gonna happen five days in a row, let alone forever.

The packaging informs the consumer that it "may take four months." Now *there's* a way to guarantee sales! "Will not work for everyone" means they've covered any possible complaints. Then

Remember how you used to pray for "thin"? Ta-da!

there's this disclaimer: "Do not apply on other parts of the body." Don't they know that we women spend our whole adult lives *removing* hair from said parts? But this was the clincher: "Stop if sudden unexpected weight gain occurs." Gosh, I'll stop before I *start*, if that's one of the possibilities.

My Plan B for hair replacement jumps right off the cover of my latest drugstore catalog with an ad that proclaims, "As Seen on TV." I feel better already. The product promises "instant hair" and is designed to "spray on in seconds, stay on until you shampoo." Which will be fifteen seconds later when you see how ridiculous you look with a spray-painted scalp. (Should you do a Rust-Oleum primer coat first?)

When I mention my thinning hair during my presentations, two things are guaranteed to happen: (1) Women in the audience will start squinting and staring very pointedly at my scalp, then turn to one another, nodding: *She's right;* and (2) Some well-meaning soul will come visit me afterward and slip a piece of paper into my hand with the name of a shampoo meant for horses (to which I say, "Neigh!"), or the telephone number of their own salon with the notation, "We can help you."

Let me say this as gently as possible: If the Lord, who created the universe and rules it as well, can't answer my prayers on this one, then I'll do what I always do when I stumble over an immovable object: laugh! Besides, as Georgia Ann, 40, has discovered, the top of your head isn't the only place where the hairs come tumbling down: "One evening as I was gazing at my reflection in the bathroom mirror, I got my old eyelash curler out of the cabinet, positioned it on my eyelid, and burst into laughter. There were no eyelashes long and strong enough to curl!"

Eyelashes can be bought, eyebrows can be drawn on (though try to avoid the perpetually "surprised" look), hats can be worn on cool days (I have six), and wigs are a distinct possibility. In another lifetime (that is, twenty-some years ago), I worked at a wig shop. Not a fancy one, the kind at the mall with the $12.95 Eva Gabor specials. In those days, the state of the art for wigs was pretty dismal. Now you can find wigs that are so real looking, if you don't know—you don't know.

I complimented a woman once who had a fabulous flip with bangs. She smiled broadly and said, "Thanks, Liz. I just had chemo, so instead of wearing a scarf I bought a wig. Sure wish mine would grow out this color!"

Well, that can be arranged (see Reason 10). And don't you love her positive outlook? She knows there's more to life than thick hair.

Maybe, instead of joining The Hairless Club for Women, I'll make the switch from bottled hair to *bought* hair. Only your wig seller knows for sure!

The Good News Is . . .

Since "the very hairs of your head are all numbered,"[6] even those of us who never got above a C in Algebra will be able to count every blessed one of ours! We'll also have less hair to wash, dry, style, comb, detangle, and color. Now if the salons would only give us a hairs-per-capita discount.

I belong to the "Birthday Bandits," a group of women who celebrate each other's birthdays. At six in the evening they picked me up to go to supper, adorned me with a rainbow wig (yes, like the clowns wear), a flashing, black over-the-hill bow tie and a black garter over my slacks. They gave me an over-the-hill whistle to wear around my neck and a mug that said, "Tease me about my age and I'll hit you with my cane." The cane came equipped with a bicycle horn, a bicycle mirror, and a rabbit's foot. Off we went to a very popular restaurant at the height of the evening supper crowd, to a table at the very center of the restaurant, to my chair adorned with several brightly colored balloons. Before the night was over I was paraded through the mall and whirled around the carousel at the food court while my friends sang "Happy Birthday," over and over and over.

Pam from Oklahoma, 40

REASON 5

Additional
pounds solve
all your winter
coat needs.

ADDITIONAL POUNDS SOLVE ALL YOUR WINTER COAT NEEDS.

Every article I've read about the over-40 body insists you must "maintain your ideal weight." "Maintain"? Hands, please, if you've ever even *achieved* your "ideal weight." Anyone? There in the back? Not too many hands.

So, perhaps you might identify with the birthday card my husband gave me (four days late) that declared, "One sign of aging is those body parts that used to stand still now start jiggling when you brush your teeth." I've heard of pricey toothpastes that whiten, brighten, bleach, treat, fight plaque, tackle tartar, massage gums, and freshen breath, but an antijiggling toothpaste? Not on the market . . . yet.

Debbie, 44, might step up to buy a tube, since she admits, "Body parts that used to be firm now jiggle like Jell-O. Therefore, as a kindergarten teacher I no longer try to teach kids to skip!"

And what part, precisely, is jiggling most on your over-40 form? "The flab under my arms," says Luan, 48. For that matter, most bodies don't wait until 40. Cindy, 47, remembers that, "When I turned 30, our young son gave me a love pat and sweetly observed, 'Mommy, your bottom feels a little bit like a water bed!'" Out of the mouths of babes—but can you spoon it back in?

Sarah from Alabama must be looking in a three-way mirror to discover this truth: "Your behind falls to nothing and your stomach becomes very well shaped and prominent. In fact, you have more coming than going!" Oh, if only it were going, going, gone.

Bob Hope had it right: "Middle age is when your age starts to show around your middle."

Some of us are scared to death to lose weight at this point in our lives for fear that our skin will sag from our bones like an old plucked turkey. Especially that under-the-chin "gobbler" look. Lynda Rae, 47, is convinced that, "If my weight disappeared, I'd be one giant wrinkle—ugh."

Pounds and inches that won't disappear sometimes change locations. When I received an invitation that said, "country western attire," I knew my favorite jean skirt just *had* to fit. Digging through the back of my closet to find my denim treasure from the summer of 1992, I finally hit pay dirt, and pulled the blue skirt into the light of day.

"Sure looks small!" I mumbled to myself, sliding it over my head. As I began to pull the straight skirt down toward my hips, now a tad more ample than the 1992 model, the truth was becoming painfully obvious. "Oh, Lord, I don't have time to shop, please let this thing fit! Even if I can't button it, Lord, at least let the zipper close!"

After ten minutes of huffing, puffing, stretching, and struggling, reality sank in: All the prayers in the world were not going to instantly add inches to my skirt, or subtract them from my hips. Off to Goodwill it went, leaving another empty skirt hanger at the Higgs house.

I'm not the only woman who's learned the hard way that some clothes need to be retired:

I went to an awards banquet wearing a floor-length, strapless tube dress with a flowing jacket. I couldn't find a strapless bra, so I settled for a black lace teddy with spaghetti straps, which remained hidden under the jacket. Felt downright slinky. When it came time to visit the ladies' room and I unsnapped the teddy, I realized I was in big trouble. There was no way on earth this big, beautiful woman was going to be able to reach around to resnap it. I went back to the party and told my husband I thought it was getting late and we should go back to our hotel, pronto. I don't think I've ever worn the teddy since.

Linda, 47

For those of us who've always been broad in the beam, the post-40 shift isn't so traumatic, but it can be devastating to women who've always been slim and trim. *What am I doing wrong?* you wonder. *Am I still walking? Yes. Still taking my vitamins? Sure. Still choosing healthy foods over Ben & Jerry's? Most of the time. Then what is the problem?* Rebecca, 46, explains it all for you: "The metabolism is shot and the weight no longer creeps onto my body, it jumps on with a vengeance."

Pam, 40, agrees: "My metabolism has not slowed down, it has stopped and is now in reverse. I have to speed past the bakery with all the windows in my car rolled up just to prevent gaining ten pounds from smelling the cinnamon rolls baking."

While we're on the subject of foodstuffs, I keep wondering how we can be gaining weight when there are so many foods that we can't even think about eating anymore? Even with a fistful of Extra Strength Tums at the ready, I can no longer consume baked beans, cole slaw, pepperoni, green peppers, or anything with cabbage in it. Ooof. Becky, 45, reminded me of another: "No more Mexican food!"

I suppose we could invest in a "Snack Alert" Refrigerator Pig. Billed as "a dieter's best friend, this chubby little porker oinks a friendly reminder whenever the refrigerator light comes on." How helpful. It has nonslip rubber feet, which means it won't fall off your fridge, but that still won't prevent you from launching the thing out the window when it oinks once too often.

Okay. The bad news is, we can't eat everything, and what we do eat will probably attach itself to our hips and thighs and fight like crazy to stay there. The good news is, the people who love us most see us through rose-colored glasses. Shirley from Pennsylvania says, "My husband still sees me as 118 pounds and 23 years old. After 34 years of marriage, I'll take it!"

Bill has learned the art of discretionary vision as well. When a slim 20-something waltzes by in short shorts, Bill shakes his head and says, "Poor thing! No meat on her bones whatsoever." Bless his heart. He knows my vulnerable spots and takes great care not to point them out.

Well, *most* of the time he takes great care. Bill and I visited my old radio station while promoting one of my books last fall. While I was in the studio, a former colleague of mine walked by and, not noticing Bill standing there, commented to another announcer, "Boy, Liz gets bigger every time I see her."

Bill cleared his throat. The fella then recognized Bill, realized his verbal faux pas, and looked for a hole to drop into. Bill wanted to cut him some slack and still stick up for me, so he said, "Yes, I'm very proud of Liz's big success!"

Cut to the car ride home. Bill told me this story, thinking I'd be very proud of his clever comeback and grateful for his support.

"He said what?" I asked, feeling faint. "That I'm 'bigger'? That can only mean one thing!"

"No, honey." Bill was backpedaling like mad by this point. "I think he was just saying that you've grown . . . uh, very popular, and . . ." Bill's goose was cooked and he knew it. The truth is, as long as my hubby thinks my 40-plus body is plus-size perfection, that's all that matters to this woman.

The Good News Is . . .

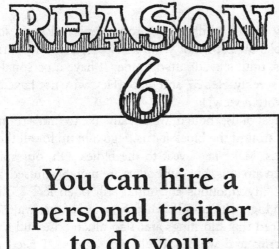

REASON
6

You can hire a
personal trainer
to do your
aerobics
for you.

YOU CAN HIRE A PERSONAL TRAINER TO DO YOUR AEROBICS FOR YOU.

My friend Audrey, 58, from New York is a *fox*. The woman looks 39, tops. For years I suspected healthy eating and good genes, until she admitted to me, "I have a personal trainer over twice weekly. He's 37 and *fine*." (Hey, why not have a workout room with a view?)

For the rest of us, though, we'd really like to find a trainer who would run around the block *for* us. Sign *him* up for all those aerobics classes. Make *her* sweat to the oldies. Oh, our spirits are willing, even anxious, but our bodies are merely amused. As Lou, 49, put it, "My emotions and mind still often feel 25, but my body gets a big kick out of it when I try to act that way."

I've noticed that mornings aren't so much "rise and shine" as they are "cries and whine." Paula, 46, agrees, "I need a jump start." Just getting physically moving is a trick. Dale, 49, says, "I used to leap out of bed, now I roll to the edge and push myself up to a sitting position. The next big challenge is to stand up and walk to the bathroom without all my bones creaking and snapping so loud that I wake up my husband!"

Speaking of sounds . . . may we? Brenda, 55, admits that "body parts I had no knowledge of have begun to groan and growl and make their location known." Pam, 44, has discovered "I'm waking up to 'snap, crackle, pop' as I climb out of bed, rather than hearing it later in my cereal bowl."

Whether we snap, crackle, pop, or worse, we all know we've got to get moving. Mikki, 54, says, "I find myself seriously considering regular exercise. Before this, my idea of exercise was to fill the tub, get in, pull the plug, and fight the current!"

"The worst thing about being over 40 is that my arms have gotten shorter!" moans Virginia from Oklahoma. "Scratching my back, touching my toes, and reading the newspaper are all much more challenging!" Nanci, 41, sighs, "Now I have to prop my foot up on the side of the tub to tie my shoe. I just can't reach the floor anymore." As Marlene Dietrich once said, "Careful grooming may take twenty years off a woman's age, but you can't fool a long flight of stairs."

I do wish I'd started some kind of regular fitness routine earlier in my life. I keep telling my children, "Start walking now! Make exercise a habit!"

They look up at me with blank expressions. "But, Mom!" they whine in unison. "Exercise isn't a habit for *you*!?"

Guilty as charged.

I really am trying. Every single day, I tell myself, "Go for a walk! Go for a walk! Take a break for ten minutes and do it!" Then when I do, I'm so worn out, I can't walk back. I start looking for neighbors to flag down and drive me home.

Bill tied on his old running shoes one evening, reminding me that, "Before we married, I used to jog five miles every night." (I fought the urge to remind him that was also the *last* time he'd gone jogging.) Before I could even figure out where I'd left off in the novel I was reading, he came panting back in the door, bug-eyed and bleeding.

His story, told between deep gulps of air, was much more dramatic than the book in my hands. He'd made it two blocks, tripped over a tree root sticking out of the sidewalk, flown through the air in middle-aged disgrace, and landed on his bum knee (all men have a bum knee, even if they never played contact sports). Dogs nearby started barking, porch lights were flicked on, and Bill hobbled home a bloody mess.

Bless his heart, the man really was in pain. I squirted some Bactine on his knee and sent him off to bed, grumbling about cracks in the sidewalk and dim street lighting.

Ann from Missouri has it right: "Pushing 40 is exercise enough!"

Some husbands lead by example. Others just push. Elaine, 40, says, "My husband has purchased the EZ Krunch and an Ab

Isolator. Get my drift?" You bet we do. Cynthia, 41, has been get-ting some prodding from her mate who "gave me $500 cash toward a treadmill. In rebellion I went out and bought some clothes!" She *did* break down, reimburse the cash, and buy the treadmill (which undoubtedly gave her a perfect place to drape all those new outfits).

The Good News Is . . .

You have lots of company. We're all creaking and groaning together. Karen, 46, put it best: "Everyone who is 40ish has the same aches and pains as you. It's a great support group. It helps to laugh together."

And isn't it handy to have a body that provides so much natu-rally funny material?

Pushing 40 is exercise enough!

I had thrown my back out and could barely move. My most comfortable position was flat on the floor with my knees bent. I'd just settled into that position when the doorbell rang, so I had to get up and was really grumpy. A young man was standing there holding a rose with a balloon attached and a card that read, "I'm sorry about your back, but I think your 40th should be one you remember. The chauffeur is waiting for you to pack and take us to the Atlanta airport to catch a plane to Cancún, Mexico." I just stood there. The young man cleared his throat and said, "Ma'am, you really need to start packing." I mumbled, "Okay," shut the door in his face, and started crying. My husband walked in with our best friends who, as it turns out, were going with us! By the time we got to Cancún, my back was the farthest thing from my mind.

Deanna from Georgia, 44

REASON 7

Less interest in
sex means more
time for
reading.

LESS INTEREST IN SEX MEANS MORE TIME
FOR READING.

Bill is a sucker for a slick brochure. Send the man to a lobby of a hotel or a doctor's waiting lounge, and he will come home with his pockets stuffed with propaganda. Usually I give him forty-eight hours to look them over before they mysteriously begin disappearing into the circular file.

But *this* brochure caught my eye: "Sexuality After 45." A question mark is implied here. I'm 42—should I be concerned? Are we talking three more years and then, *poof*, no more love life? The pamphlet goes on to suggest that "hot flashes and night sweats may lessen your desire for sex." So can toddlers who wake up screaming at midnight, but why let something like that dampen your spirits?

Years of familiarity can take their toll, no doubt. Carolyn, 47, shares: "I especially miss the feeling of romance that only comes back occasionally. I love my husband of twenty-five years very much, but I miss the physical excitement that was so much a part of our lives. Yes, the love has deepened, and we have grown closer, but I miss the yesterdays." It is discouraging when your husband turns out the lights for economic reasons rather than romantic ones.

When Bill and I were dating, he sent me an expensive greeting card *every single day* during the four months before our wedding. Now when we go browsing through greeting card racks, he shows me his favorites, asks me to read them, then carefully slips them back on the rack without bending the corners. "Hope you liked them!" he purrs. "I picked those out just for you!"

Reading is exactly what many of us turn to when bedtime beckons and our mate doesn't. Not to worry, this solution has been around for centuries: "That night the king could not sleep;

so he ordered the book of the chronicles, the record of his reign, to be brought in and read to him."[7] See? Even King Ahasuerus burned the midnight oil with a book by his side.

Not every over-40 couple is spending their time in bed reading, of course. Sandra, 47, thinks the good news about being over 40 is you're "old enough to know better and young enough to still wanta!" It appears Patty, 44, and her hubby are still young enough to "wanta": "One day our 15-year-old son came down the stairs and caught my husband and me 'necking' on the couch. He shouted out (in a rather loud voice), 'Oooh, old people kissing! You shouldn't do that in front of children!'" At our house, Bill and I smooch a lot in front of the kids, so they know how wonderfully romantic marriage can be!

Thanks in part to slinky young screen stars and romance novels with nubile, 20-something heroines, we often assume that when we say "so long" to our 20s, we're waving good-bye to romance as well. Diane from Ohio knows better: "When I turned 30, I was depressed because I thought I was an old maid and had lost my youth and chance for romance. A year later I celebrated my birthday on my honeymoon with my Mr. Honey! You never know what God has in store for you."

I was almost 32, and Bill nearly 34, when we married, so if you're single and longing for romance, don't despair—it could happen! For those who are married but missing some zip, Candy, 48, points out that "I feel better than I did when I was 25 because I've learned the value of good nutrition and exercise. Sex is better than ever!"

Even if you're not as agile as you used to be, doing loving things for one another can bring its own kind of pleasure. What woman wouldn't like to have a hubby like Georgia's?

I can no longer give myself a pedicure as I used to.
But there's a silver lining in this dark cloud. My darling
hubby now takes one foot at a time and pampers me
with his clipping and indulging. Now I can't wait until I

need a "foot job" and enjoy it more than I ever imagined.

Georgia, 40

Makes my toes curl to think about it! The surest way to put a little zip in your love life is to get away with your mate for an evening with just the two of you, alone. One year, for example, I decided I'd kidnap Bill for Valentine's Day. No ransom note pasted together from newspaper headlines, though, since it was unlikely his parents would hand over a cool grand just to get their 40-something son back from the clutches of his love-crazed wife.

When I let the children in on my plans, they weren't as excited about the just-Mom-and-Dad guest list.

"Why can't we go?" Lillian whined.

"Yeah!" Matthew joined in. "We could take our sleeping bags and stay in the same room with you guys!"

Oh brother. I gently explained that just this once Mom and Dad would be traveling alone.

"Whyyyy?" Lillian moaned, turning one syllable into a kindergarten siren.

"Because we love each other and need some time to . . . be together," I replied, stumbling for the right words.

By 6:45 on the Big Night, I was ready, and all three of us were antsy. I watched the driveway with one eye and the clock with the other. Where was that baby-sitter? She simply had to get there before Bill did or the kidnapping would lose its most vital element: Surprise.

When she pulled into our driveway just seconds before 7:00, the Zero Hour, I practically dragged her through the front door, stammered through my last-minute instructions, grabbed our suitcase, and headed for the van. No sooner had I started the engine and popped a Vivaldi cassette into the tape player, when Bill pulled in behind the baby-sitter's car.

The look of confusion on his face turned to concern, even panic, as I marched toward him, yanked open his door, and said with a straight face, "This way, please, and no questions."

"Huh?" he said, catching a glimpse of two children with wide-eyed faces pressed tightly against the front window. "What about the kids? What's going on?" He was slowly turning the color of his pink dress shirt.

I grabbed a blindfold and extended it toward him. "Put it on, please." An hour later, sixty miles from home, I yanked off his blindfold with a flourish. "Here we are! Quilted Memories Bed & Breakfast. Doesn't it look romantic?"

"Sure," he said climbing out. I could tell he wasn't sure at all. Only a dim porch bulb suggested we were expected. We pushed the doorbell and waited. And waited. Finally, a cross-looking woman appeared, gave us a stern stare between the lace curtains, then unlocked the door and opened it just enough for us to slide in.

"The natives are not very friendly," Bill whispered, and we giggled as we headed up the stairs toward our room. I held my breath when I opened the door and was relieved to discover the room was much more inviting than its owner.

"How 'bout I take a quick shower?" Bill suggested as I unpacked. *Maybe this night can be salvaged after all*, I thought, hanging our clothes up in the antique wardrobe.

Bill's "quick shower" turned into the usual thirty-minute hot water extravaganza. At last, he dripped his way back into our room, warm and wet and freshly shaved. "Nice," I said, brushing his cheek and flashing my most beguiling smile. "I'll be right back."

Alas, my ten-minute bird bath was still too long. When I tiptoed into our room, I found Bill snoring soundly in our king-size bed. Drooling even, the covers tucked under his chin like a little boy who's had a long week.

Ah, well, I thought, reaching for my purse. *Mornings are nice, too. Now, where is that romance novel?*

The Good News Is . . .

Sex after 40 is more fun. That is to say, you laugh a lot more in bed. The agility of your 20s and the intensity of your 30s have given way to the levity of your 40-plus bodies. Ron, 48, has noticed "all the strange new sounds you discover your body making. The wife and I lie in bed sometimes and laugh hysterically at the things we hear ourselves doing."

You read it here first.

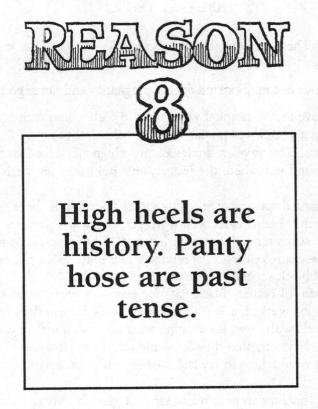

REASON
8

High heels are
history. Panty
hose are past
tense.

HIGH HEELS ARE HISTORY. PANTY HOSE
ARE PAST TENSE.

There are four things nobody told me about the maturing foot:

1. Your feet may expand during pregnancy and never go back.

I drove to the hospital wearing an 8½ shoe and came home wearing a 10B. I was prepared for my old clothes not to fit, but my *shoes*? The swollen ankles of my pregnancy receded and I soon found out where the water went: right into my heels and toes.

Imagine disposing of an entire closet floor full of shoes, some so new they hadn't even been worn yet. The worst part was having Bill watch me pull box after box out of the closet. He'd never seen the entire collection at a whack like that. "Who needs five pairs of black shoes?" he whined in exasperation.

We do, of course. Black flats for everyday wear, plain black pumps for work, black patent leather heels for Sundays, black high heels with bows for evening wear and black loafers for . . . loafing. Hey, I figured they'd last me for years. How did I know my feet would grow in my late 30s? My earlobes, maybe, but my *feet*?

The Israelites weren't ready for foot growth either: "Nor did your foot swell these forty years,"[8] but after that, look out!

2. Your toes will get ugh-ly.

Multiple decades of high heels have reshaped our feet into a knotty pile of permanent lumps and bumps. Those aren't corns, they're our toes. I found an ad for a device that "removes calluses and corns safely and quickly." Yes, speed is of the essence here. Don't you hate those trimmers that take hours? This one handles "troublesome foot growths with minimal effort" and comes with *"thirteen* reversible stainless-steel blades." Sounds unlucky. Even dangerous. Like having dinner at a Japanese restaurant where they throw all those knives around, except you'd put your feet on the table instead of a beef steak. Ouch! I'll just keep my lumpy toes, thanks.

3. High heels will have less appeal.

When I disposed of all the shoes in my closet, I noticed an interesting phenomenon: The shoes that went out had two-inch heels; the new shoes that replaced them had one-inchers, max. When those wore out, the next generation had almost no heels at all. Now I'm wearing what amount to ballet shoes with rubber soles.

I consider this a sign of intellectual growth.

High heels are for younger women whose ankles still bend without breaking and whose fashion sense demands that elevated look. Out of respect for the gravity that is slowly but surely pulling me downward, I have chosen to retire my tippy-toe shoes for good. I think Job's friends were right: "A trap seizes him by the heel; a snare holds him fast."[9] I am ensnared no more.

Flats are also fashionable again—still—and I think I know why. The designers couldn't bear watching us trot to work in their pricey suits and silk blouses paired with huge neon-striped running shoes. That's why they designed high heels that were supposed to be as comfortable as sneakers and showed grown women playing basketball in them.

Nice try. Give us our flats, and we'll go away quietly.

I've made another delightful discovery: "Cushioning Comfort Insoles with Sure Grip Foam." I wore one foamy pair for a day and was back at the store the next morning trying to purchase them in case lots.

4. The changes won't stop at your ankle bone.

Here's another fine mess my body has gotten me into. I now have red blotches around my ankles. If I wear bobby socks you can't see them, so with just the right length skirt (well below the knees) and properly positioned socks, my legs still look youthful in some lighting situations. Twilight, for instance.

Even in flats, with comfy socks and foam pads in place, our feet aren't safe from every disaster. Brenda had a birthday experience that painfully demonstrates the agony of de feet: "My husband had a surprise party for me in our condo and asked me to make punch (figure that!). I dropped a half-gallon bottle of cranberry juice on my big toe and broke it—the toe, not the bottle. I sat through my party in agony, and as soon as everyone left, off to the ER I went!"

Since the over-40 woman is built for comfort and not for speed, we not only want happy feet, we want happy legs as well. For many of us, our taste in panty hose has changed as we matured. In our teens, we wore fishnet stockings, textured stripes, and zippy colors. In our 20s we sported one-size-fits-all, bare-toe-to-waist panty hose in the sheerest styles allowed by law. Then in our 30s, control-top hose began to offer more appeal, as did reinforced toes and heels.

These days, we want an ultrasupport model that camouflages a multitude of red and blue lines, puts some pep into our step, and holds everything from waist to knees in a seemingly flab-free position. (Who said anything about breathing?) The problem with those spandex support hose is the gyrations you put yourself through to get them on. Lisa from North Carolina frets over "getting panty hose over your hips without throwing your back out."

Which is why many of us these days have quietly started skipping the beasties altogether in favor of an updated old favorite: knee-highs. Not only the cable-knit numbers in the winter, but the sheer-to-the-toe variety in warmer weather. They're a natural with slacks, but lots of us get away with them under dresses as well. WARNING: Your dress needs to be almost ankle length to pull this off without anyone knowing you're "cheating." One stiff breeze and we'll see your knees!

The Good News Is . . .

As a woman grows older, her judgment gets better;
She cares how her shoes fit instead of her sweater!

Jean Boyce

After 40, it's harder to see your feet anyway. Who cares if they're a tad wider, or your shoes are flatter, or your hose start at your knees? If you can put one foot in front of the other and keep moving, you're one lucky dame.

The night before my birthday, I celebrated with friends, dancing and having a great time. The next day, my parents and sister were planning to take me to lunch at my favorite eatery. I received flowers and the day was going great. Suddenly I felt an ache in my lower back and thought I had pulled a muscle while dancing. The ache spread and I was in so much pain I had to ask a coworker to take me to the clinic. On the way to the car I passed my father pulling into my office and told him to follow us to the clinic, where I found out I was having a kidney stone attack. Meanwhile, my siblings were at my office with a bunch of clowns they'd hired to play the "Death March" on kazoos! When my dad told them that I was sick, they took pictures of the clowns and came to the clinic to check on me. I'm not sure who was the most disappointed!

Dale from Illinois, 49

REASON
9

The most
flattering
bathing suit is
a beach towel
with shoulder
straps.

THE MOST FLATTERING BATHING SUIT IS A BEACH TOWEL WITH SHOULDER STRAPS.

"Bathing Suit Season" is a loaded term. It doesn't just mean June, July, and August, or a week at the Jersey shore. It implies long legs, a golden tan, curves without bulges, a few well-placed freckles, and one very flat stomach.

The bathing suit has clout. No other article of clothing has its own season. We don't talk about "Gored Skirt Season," or "Cotton Blouse Season." But the lowly bathing suit, made from half a yard of fabric, carries so much social significance that it has practically replaced the word *summer.*

On television, bathing suits are on display year-round. Karen, 44, finds one of the fun things about life after 40 is "watching *Baywatch* and laughing hysterically! All that silicone and steroid-pumped flesh . . . is this show FDA approved?"

The problem is, bathing suits have no mercy. They hide nothing. Let's face it, they are little more than printed undergarments. Bras with stripes. Panties with pizzazz.

We, who used to run down the hallway shrieking if our older brother saw us in our underwear, happily paraded down a crowded beach later that afternoon, wearing even less.

Cindy, 43, had a stroll along Laguna Beach with a friend that produced a memorable conversation:

A perky little blonde buzzed up to us on her roller blades. She was quite chipper in explaining to us that she was working with Gillette to market a new deodorant and her mission was to put samples of this product into the hands of all who fit their very well-defined market. She handed us our samples and as she roller-bladed into the hot Laguna sun, she babbled, "Be sure

to tell all your friends about our new deodorant." The
name of the product was "Teen Spirit."

All I can say is, Cindy must do more for a bathing suit than I ever did. One-piece swimsuits came in two styles when I was growing up. Either it was made out of armor-thick nylon and elastic (think "foundation"), with layers of ruffles and wraps (as if to say, "There is nothing under here but more fabric." Wink. Wink).

Or, it wasn't really a one-piece suit at all, but rather a three-quarter suit, cut out with geometric vengeance, producing circles of sunburn in strange places.

The sixties also gave us the topless bathing suit. Really, Rudi Gernreich, what were you thinking of? Comediennes of the era had a field day. Carol Burnett said she tried a peekaboo bathing suit: People took one peek and said, "Boo." Phyllis Diller described standing on the beach for hours in a topless bathing suit, until she finally got arrested. For loitering. The policeman kept calling her "Mac."

My friend Karla found the perfect way to improve your appearance in a bathing suit: Just raise your arms, pull in your tummy, and lose fifteen years! Of course, that means walking around all day looking as if you're about to dive into the pool, but what price vanity?

Jean from Washington spent her 40th birthday in her bathing suit (as opposed to her birthday suit!): "It was a surprise party at my girlfriend's place. I was invited down for a swim in her pool and so showed up in just a bathing suit and towel to find a patio full of friends. Quite a surprise!" Being the only person at my own party in a bathing suit would do me in! A few months ago, I ventured out in the first bathing suit I'd worn in public in a long time. Swimming at a hotel pool in far-away-from-home Colorado Springs, I found out several exciting things:

1. Nobody looked.
2. Nobody cared.

Your figure is still terrific.
Especially if you stand on your head.

3. Without glasses or contact lenses, I couldn't see their reaction anyway!

I was so jazzed after the joy of splashing around like a kid again, that I took an even braver step and went to a huge public water park, *not* so far from home but still a safe ninety miles away. I took off my ankle-length cover-up and waited for uproarious laughter. Once again, nobody looked, nobody cared, and I couldn't see 'em . . . whee! Alas, I was not quite as far away from Louisville as I needed to be—three different women at the Wave Pool shouted out, "Aren't you Liz Curtis Higgs?" No way around it: That's me. The good news is, the other 972 people there didn't recognize the name—or me—so why sweat it? Jump into the pool and be cool!

The Good News Is . . .

You really aren't concerned about attracting the attention of that bronzed hunk of a lifeguard anyway. Frankly, he'll only notice you if you're drowning. Youngsters will *not* do belly flops at the sight of your cellulite, honest. They may laugh behind their hands, but they do that watching *America's Funniest Home Videos,* so clearly their tastes are skewed.

Finally, who cares if you look as though you were poured into your suit and forgot to say "when"? If it covers the basics and lets you play in the water, that's what matters most!

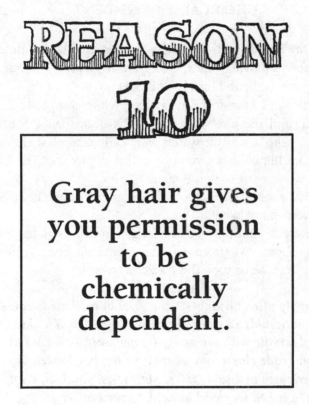

REASON 10

Gray hair gives
you permission
to be
chemically
dependent.

GRAY HAIR GIVES YOU PERMISSION TO BE CHEMICALLY DEPENDENT.

My friend Judith from Oregon says that by the time you hit 40, you're moving into the Metallic Age: silver in your hair, gold in your teeth, and lead in your feet.

In my case, I have foam in my feet, white composite stuff in my teeth, and the only gray hairs I have are below the scalp because I keep a vigilant watch with Lady Clairol at the ready. Lynda from Illinois has given up on that approach: "The Clairol stopped working. It took too many bottles."

Juli, 39, is a soul sister, too: "Gray hair and chin hair are starting to overrun my head!"

There are several options here. Mary from New Jersey is still deciding about "when to let the gray hair come through." Margaret from Texas took the sneaky approach:

Shortly after turning 40, the gray in my hair became more noticeable so I began to have it frosted. Thinking I looked terrific with my newly frosted hair, I entered a second-grade classroom where a young boy looked at me curiously and said, "Mrs. Matthews, you look a lot older." I asked why and he said, "Your hair is getting white." I told him I paid good money to make my hair look that way! He looked at me again and said, "Yeah, well you've got wrinkles, too." Maybe I can get my wrinkles frosted?

I've heard of Frosted Flakes, but frosted wrinkles don't sound very appealing. Barbara admits that "since I turned 40, it seems I have to frost my hair less often because of the beautiful frosting job that the Lord is giving me. I just wish that the color He was frosting it with was the same color I've been using all along!"

Although "the silver-haired head is a crown of glory,"[10] Dale from Illinois doesn't think it's so glorious. "I have spent many moments plucking the gray hairs around my hair line, but who knows what I'm missing in the back! Then I noticed a gray hair in my eyebrow—do I pluck or use more eyebrow pencil?"

What? Give up a perfectly healthy eyebrow hair? Revlon to the rescue! I just wish they made eyebrow pencils to match your hair coloring lotion. Wouldn't it be grand if hair coloring kits came with coordinating eyebrow pencils taped to the lid, "Free with Purchase"?

I love to ask women in my audience, "How many of you have no idea what your natural hair color is?" Honest hands pop up all over the room, followed by gasps from their friends who never knew the truth. These are women who, like me, started out using "Sun-In" at the pool during the sixties, then graduated to Lady Clairol 121, and finally switched to L'Oreal because we're worth it.

I sported blonde locks for the first forty years of my life, but found that the blonde and the gray were starting to fight for attention up there. Now, along with thousands of other American women, I've opted for red hair this season and am delighted with the results. Why be salt-and-pepper when you can be paprika?

I'm also wearing it longer than I used to. Maybe I'm merely following the apostle Paul's directive: "If a woman has long hair, it is a glory to her; for her hair is given to her for a covering."[11] Or, it could be my thinning hair situation. I'm moving my part farther and farther to the left so I have plenty to comb over my sparse spot, just as the guys do. (Hey, fellas, at least I'm not combing it all into one big swirl on top!)

Not that we don't play a few games of our own in the stylist's chair, like insisting we want it cut to chin length. "Since I have three chins, I have about six inches I can work with," admits Sarah from Tennessee.

Marian, 45, is a Native American who has found that long hair has its own set of challenges:

As a young wife, I had long black hair. When you have small children, it becomes bothersome, pulled, and in the way. To my husband's dismay, I had it cut repeatedly until there was almost none left. Now that I'm more mature (and sexy) I decided to let my hair grow long once again. Guess what? It becomes bothersome, pulled, and in the way. I told a friend at work that I wanted to be an old Indian with a long braid. She told me, "Marian, you are an old Indian whether you have a braid or not!"

My husband is delighted with my slightly longer locks, but my hairdresser is fighting me every inch of the way. Every six weeks, her scissors are poised over my head, the gleaming shears reflecting the predatory look in her eyes. She wants that hair. Can almost feel it snip-snipping beneath her lightning-fast shears, falling to the floor in pitiful wisps. She murmurs something about it "being for my own good," insisting that thin and long don't make a good combination. Good news: Going with the red-headed look has made my stylist so happy that she's stopped harping about cutting it.

Maybe she grew up with the same messages that Pamela from South Carolina did, telling her "I should cut my hair because my mother's generation said you looked cheap over 40 with long hair. My hair is long and blonde and I'm 42. I love it this way but constantly fight the 'little voice.'"

Tell the little voice to take a little hike. After 40, you can wear your hair very short or very long, very gray or any color in the rainbow, without worrying about looking too young or too cheap. Cheap? On the contrary. If you can drop sixty dollars to chase that gray away, you're old enough to choose your own hair color and whip out a Platinum AmEx to pay for it.

The Good News Is . . .

Glenda from Georgia took her silvering 40-something mane to the Bahamas with her husband. "We played and shopped and acted like 18 year olds. I thought, *How lucky I am that he loves my baggy body and graying hair.*"

Well, of course he does, because that graying hair springs from a head that still knows how to act 18. Lucky him!

Effective immediately, let's start calling them *silver* hairs, not gray. Gray conjures up images of dark, gloomy days and boring business suits. Silver sounds much more eye-catching: silver dollars, silver certificates, sterling silver, silver jewelry. Instead of coloring our hair, let's just polish it!

When my friend Carmen turned 40, we had a party for ten at her house that evening. Then when everyone was leaving at midnight, three of us whipped out sleeping bags for a slumber party. We'd bought two dozen rolls of toilet paper to put all over her yard and were on our hands and knees crawling backward out of the room when Carmen woke up. She wanted to go to the local cafe for coffee but we had to stall her because we had people coming there for cake at 8:00. Later we had three guys duct-tape Carmen to a desk chair on wheels, attach helium balloons, put a party hat on her head, and wheel her around town in the rain. That night at her daughter's basketball game, we came out on center court dressed as old people, announced her birthday, and made her dance with us on the gym floor. Carmen's picture (we were unrecognizable in masks) made the paper!

Leigh from North Dakota, 42

REASON

11

You can finally sell that prom dress at the consignment shop.

11

YOU CAN FINALLY SELL THAT PROM DRESS AT THE CONSIGNMENT SHOP.

Junior Year, 1971: My date for the prom was Bill. No, not *my* Bill, another one. This Bill had skinny freckled arms, wiry hair, and buckteeth. (Look, I was just grateful somebody asked me.)

My only clear memory of prom night was sitting in the car outside my parents' house where Bill threw up on my dress. It needed it. Dark, pine-needle green with white, three-dimensional daisies popping out all over it—my dress looked like a lawn gone to seed.

That prom dress didn't end up at the consignment shop, it ended up in the trash can. As ugly as it was, I wish I had it in my closet for Lillian to enjoy, because as any fashion magazine will tell you, the sixties are back with a vengeance. Frances, 42, says, "Kids think I'm cool when I show them the pink suede over-the-knee boots and miniskirt I used to wear." Ooh, pink suede, very "Hullabaloo." Ruth, 43, loves watching her 16-year-old son "digging through our closets looking for bell-bottoms and hip-huggers." And Cindy says, "The teenagers I work with were totally astounded to learn that I was alive back when tie-dye was popular the first time."

If you're over 40, you remember what came *before* bell-bottoms and tie-dyes: kilts. No, not like in Scotland, with sporrans and bagpipes. These were the Ladybug and Villager varieties, worn with heavy cable-knit sweaters so that when we got two blocks away from home, we could roll the skirts up a notch or two under our bulky sweaters. Sure, it gave us the waist of a grandmother, but at least we had the legs of a miniskirted fashion model.

Mother's hem rules were firm: The skirt *had* to come to my fingertips. Stand up a moment, arms at your side, and you'll see what she was letting me get away with. My, how times have changed. Now my own rule for skirt length is: Reveal as little of my blotchy ankles as possible.

I've been pushing for longer hems since the first moon landing. I was the first girl at Warwick High to wear a midi-skirt. I was also the *only* girl at Warwick High to wear a midi-skirt. Made of heavy polyester (what else, in 1971?), my ivory and navy novelty hit midcalf, revealing legs clad in navy ribbed stockings and platform shoes. Very Carnaby Street. It's the only item of clothing I've saved for twenty-five years. If dresses were like cars, it would qualify as an antique.

The other big fashion trend that we 40-plusers remember coming into vogue was the two-piece pantsuit. Oh, weren't *they* a prize when they first appeared. Heavy textured polyester (again) with a tunic that quit at the most unflattering spot on our hips, paired with matching slacks that were neither stovepiped nor bell-bottomed, they just ended at our ankles. Of course, we thought they were wonderfully wrinkle-free and so slimming— all one color, head to toe, just as the editors of *Seventeen* insisted.

We stopped wearing two-piece pantsuits the minute our mothers discovered them.

My own mother thought fashion was just so much vain foolishness. She had one ensemble that sufficed anytime a dress was called for: a white cotton shirtwaist with a knife-pleated full skirt that swirled when she walked, dotted with green and orange circles that looked like olives. For weddings and such, she added a white hat with an orange and green bow and smashing tangerine high heels. Very Loretta Young. I bought an almost identical dress—less the olives—in 1987, a mere thirty years later. Mom would've loved it.

The Good News Is . . .

If the fashion wheel continues to spin around at the same speed, by the time we hit the Big 5-0, we'll be wearing solid navy suits again with little floppy bow ties and plain navy pumps, looking like aging flight attendants who can't remember where we stowed our roasted peanuts. So, if you haven't dragged *those* old favorites to the consignment shop yet, just tuck them into the back of the closet. You'll be all set to wow your grandchildren in 2007!

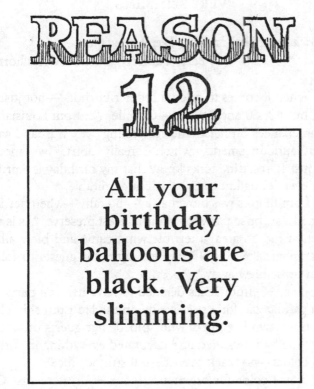

REASON 12

All your birthday balloons are black. Very slimming.

ALL YOUR BIRTHDAY BALLOONS ARE BLACK.
VERY SLIMMING.

The trick about birthdays is to keep having them.
                    Barry Bernson, WHAS-TV Anchorman

When it comes to celebrating her birthday—not just the Big 4-0, but 50, 60 and 70, too—Camille, 72, from Louisiana is taking no chances on her friends forgetting. "My husband says I send out announcements, which I really don't. Two months ahead I just start letting folks know that my birthday is April 2." See, she even let us know! Sneaky, but admirable.

Janet from Illinois was blown away—literally—when her family planned a surprise party for her at a forest preserve. "As is normal in the Chicago area, a terrible wind came and blew all the party paraphernalia away!! They left signs for guests to follow, and even those blew away."

Mary Jane, 46, from Texas decided to have her *own* party. She rented a paddleboat for a sunset ride on the Houston ship channel and hired two bagpipers who "piped" her guests on and off the boat. She had it catered and decorated everything in "bright, cheerful colors—no black over-the-hill stuff for me!"

Black is *the* color for celebrating your 40th, it seems. Card shops carry a whole array of gift items for each major "zero" birthday, and without exception, 40 is draped in black. Ellen, 43, remembers "a kitchen full of hundreds of black balloons that greeted me first thing in the morning, and the large six-inch button that my family made me wear all day that said, '39 Forever.'"

Jane from Indiana was conducting her church choir on her big day. "As the choir members began arriving for rehearsal, it didn't register with me that everyone was dressed in the same color. As I gave a downbeat to start warm-ups, it took every bit of self-control I could muster to not burst out laughing at all the black." Jill, 48, took the initiative on her birthday, and "wore all black to work and started calling myself an 'Aging Love Goddess.'"

Not everyone looks good in black, of course. Pat from Utah was adorned with all the usual on her 40th: "Black ribbons, banners, balloons, cake, and so on. A 5-year-old neighbor boy who is a dear friend of mine threw a fit about all the ugly black. He brought me a rainbow balloon all by himself so I'd have something 'pretty' for my birthday and then asked if he could 'kill' all the black balloons!"

Madline, 42, undoubtedly had a few murderous thoughts of her own when her new brother-in-law, a funeral director, "had a funeral preplan packet made up with a special 'In Memory Of' card. The 'Place' of the memorial service was listed as a local mental health facility, my father-in-law was named as the 'Clergyman' (which he isn't), and the 'Place of Interment' was the 'Over the Hill Cemetery.'"

I found two stories in Scripture that might shed some light on why funeral themes are so popular. On Pharaoh's birthday, the guest of honor hung his chief baker. At Herod's party, the birthday boy presented a dancing fool with John the Baptist's head on a platter. Talk about over the edge!

Peggy, 46, another choir director, was nervous about her 40th "since I had royally roasted everyone who turned 40 before I did. But my dear pastor husband assured me no one would notice. Little did I know what was waiting for me in the fellowship hall. Black balloons, black cake, and a singing telegram delivering a funeral dirge."

Music is a popular addition to 40th fun, and we're not just talking "Happy Birthday to You." Ann, 43, sat in a rocking chair to open her presents "while two guys sang 'The Old Gray Mare.'" And at Melinda's 40th, "a gorilla danced and we had a family gathering." As I understand it, only one of her relatives is a gorilla.

For Ardith's big surprise doings at the church hall, her husband displayed posters with her photos from over the years. If

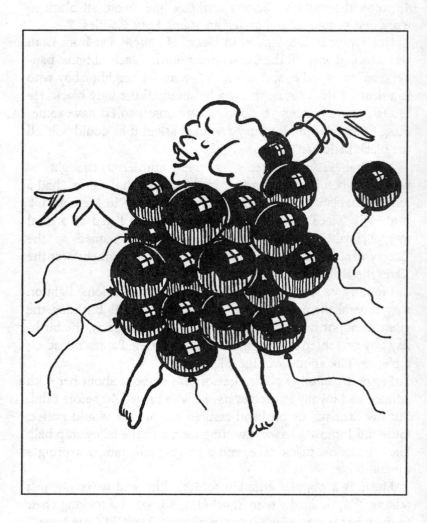

Black is a slimming color.
On a penguin.

my Bill pulled a stunt like that, the surprise would be on him: I wouldn't show up! "Here's Liz in eighth grade with pointy cat glasses and braces. Here's Liz in tenth grade . . . ooh, a thin year! Here's Liz in her senior graduation photo, sporting the worst shag haircut ever inflicted on a woman in Lancaster County, Pennsylvania."

At a recent family reunion, each of us was presented with our senior portrait. After two dozen years of hanging in my parents' home, it was time for me to get stuck with it. We're talking ugly. Sixteen by twenty inches of black-and-white Liz, painted in colors meant to approximate real life. Bill, who once supported himself as a photographer, says the process is called "tinting," meaning they jot down a few reminders while you're in the studio—blue eyes, blonde hair—then guess in the darkroom.

Yes, my eyes are sparkling blue, the dimples are definitely there, but that haircut is still the pits. The layered style we called a "shag" had just hit town in 1972, and the hairdresser at Betty's Beauty Parlor was dying to give it a go. The day before my photo session, I bravely surrendered my shoulder-length hair to her scissors, not knowing that one dumb decision would haunt me in color-tinted horror for decades to follow. The shag: a great dance, an iffy carpet, a horrible haircut (which, of course, is back in style). The shaggy Liz photo won't make an appearance at my next birthday, or any other day.

If 40 is still on your horizon, take it from those who've gone before you: Hide all your old photos, wear bright colors, avoid funeral homes, and when they shout, "Surprise," don't lose your head!

The Good News Is . . .

Black balloons aren't the only thing you might get on your 40th. Connie from California was given "a surprise chocolate shower!" Yummy. On her 50th, Lynn from Arkansas received "an old, faded flour sack filled with something that weighed very little but made a rustling noise: fifty brand-new dollar bills, all crinkled up . . . such fun to open!" Even more fun to spend.

One party featured disposable cameras on every table, encouraging folks to take pictures, then leave the cameras for the host to develop. Clever, eh? Here's another genuinely thoughtful gift, since candles are so "hot" these days: Fill a pretty gift box with forty candles in different styles, colors, and scents.

Even with all the black decor, your 40th can be a blast. Sally, 46, relates, "There was a small nudging voice telling me I should be depressed, but I was having too much fun to listen." In fact, Judy, 42, says, "The week I turned 40 started with a big surprise party thrown by my husband, then a week of lunches with friends, and finally a party with my relatives. Turning 41 was a real disappointment!"

Maybe that's just as well. At our age, we can only handle so much excitement. After painting the town red, we may need a good nap before applying a second coat. Gentlewomen, clean your paintbrushes . . . 50 is next!

I was on vacation with my family on Kiawah Island, South Carolina. Being away from home lulled me into a false sense of safety from the usual "you're 40" pranks. My family sent my husband and me to the store for supplies. We returned to yard signs of "Lordy, Lordy, Doris is 40" and were greeted by my nephew with a video camera. There was black crepe paper everywhere, "40" plates, posters, black roses, and an "over-the-hill" gift at my place at the table. I retreated momentarily to my room, followed by the video man, where I found a big "40" on the wall over my bed and more black crepe paper on lamps, mirrors, and walls. They must have been saving it since Halloween. I realized how much they loved me to bring all this stuff on vacation—they gave up a whole carton of supplies just to surprise me!

Doris from Kentucky, 44

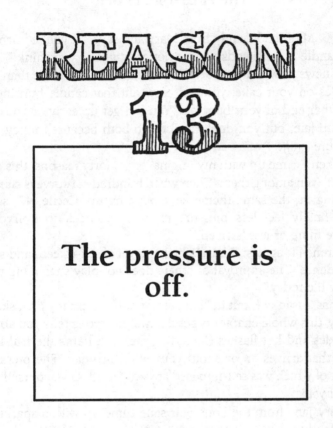

REASON 13

The pressure is off.

13

THE PRESSURE IS OFF

My friend Candy from Maryland says, "If you're burning the candle at both ends, you're not as bright as you think!" The good news is, when you turn 40 you can blow out more than the candles on your cake; you can blow out that candle burning at the other end of your busy day. You can get up early or you can stay up late, but you don't need to do both because, honey, the pressure is *off*.

When I came up with my original list of forty reasons, this one wasn't even among them. Then when hundreds of surveys started pouring in, the same theme kept popping up. Cecile, 42, said, "You finally feel less pressure to prove yourself to everyone. You've more or less 'arrived.'"

Karen, 41, agrees: "I have a higher level of self-esteem and self-confidence. The approval of others does not play such a big part in my life today."

Or as Susan, 44, put it, "I'm comfortable within my own skin."

Say, this whole chapter is good news! Everyone tells you about wrinkles and hot flashes (including me), but here's the *real* surprise that arrives on or about your 40th birthday: The pressure (most of which was self-imposed anyway) is off. Give yourself the gift of *you!*

Mary Jane from the Lone Star state came up with a sparkling idea for her youngest sister's 40th: "I tapped her with a beribboned wand and told her the 'Forty Fairy' gave her permission to quit putting up with some in-law garbage. We started laughing and naming all sorts of things she no longer had to do now that she was 40. Finally, she felt so liberated she decided the Forty Fairy was her favorite present!"

Men experience this wonder of life after 40, too. David, 45, admits, "I can get away with more!" And Ron, 41, realizes "I'm now at a time in my life when I don't have to worry about impressing anyone. Actually, it's too late to impress anyone!"

Sandy from Pennsylvania offers a positive spin on things: "One thing about being homely all your life—you don't have to worry about 'losing it' when you get old. So *there*, Cindy Crawford!"

Even Cindy will have to face 40 someday, but for her, the pressure will never be off. Think of that! Her fame and fortune have so revolved around her looks that until they take her away in a pine box, people will be commenting on her appearance. Celebrities in general, and especially female ones, never have the freedom that you and I have just to "be." Elizabeth Taylor's figures have been more closely watched than the stock market. Oprah's ratings have gone up and down and so has her scale, all observed by the unforgiving eye of the viewing public.

Lucky us! Nobody is watching. I mean *nobody*. The pressure began lifting at 30, moving off so slowly, so quietly, that we almost didn't notice. Suddenly, at 40 we became aware of this new freedom and a whole new set of (lower) expectations:

> When *you're young, society rates women 1–10, the question being, "How close to a Perfect 10 can you come?" But once you're 40, society seems to rate women 1–10 on how much above a "1" you can get. As in, "She looks great, for 40. She has a good figure, for 40." The pressure is off! Now we can shoot for a "Perfect 1"!*
>
> **Pamela, 42**

Jeanne from California laughingly says, "I no longer give any thought to whether or not my purse matches my shoes. I can't believe how much of my younger years was spent worrying about what others would think." Arline thinks that freedom goes beyond appearance: "You can say things you've never had the nerve to say before, because age has its privileges."

I got a firsthand glimpse of the over-40 attitude in action a dozen years ago when my sister Sarah (I was 28 then to her 40) and I went to a very nice restaurant in Louisville. The line to the ladies' room was long and slow (what's new?), but the men's room seemed deserted.

"Cover me!" Sarah said, and ducked into the doorway marked *Men.*

Cover her? What is this, a James Bond movie? I was beyond embarrassed and ran to our table to wait for her, hoping no one noticed that we were even together. Today, I would've been the first one to whip open the door and say, "We're coming in!"

The Good News Is . . .

When we let go of judging others, we also let go of judging ourselves. Losses and changes have taught us the value of appreciation and gratitude. So what if we don't look as good as we did at 20? We are thinking and acting *much better!*

Lois, 40, from Montana agrees: "I'm less worried about the look of the container, and have more freedom to devote to the care and well-being of the contents inside—namely, me! I'm dressing my soul, not just my body."

Cathy, 40, a self-proclaimed compulsive perfectionist, poses an important question whenever she makes a mistake: "I ask myself, 'Will anyone remember this in a year?' No way. Most of us can't remember what we did yesterday!"

As a wise man once said, "That which is has already been, / And what is to be has already been."[12] Or, as Doris Day put it, "Que Sera, Sera!"

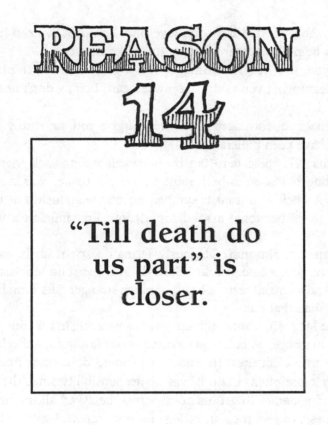

REASON 14

"Till death do us part" is closer.

"TILL DEATH DO US PART" IS CLOSER.

You married him. You love him. You plan to keep him. Unless he pulls another birthday stunt like last year.

Maybe, like Bill, he didn't get you a present at all, thinking you meant what you said: "Gee, sweetheart, I really don't need a thing . . ."

Then again, considering what he *did* give you, an empty box might have been preferable.

Diana, 47, spent her 40th birthday celebrating with friends, including her soon-to-be hubby, whose gift to her was . . . a brick. A *brick*? "He said it symbolized our relationship at that point—a cornerstone, a solid foundation. Romantic in a way, eh?"

Romantic? Hm-mm. Obviously, Diana doesn't read the same romance novels I do. A *brick*? But I do like that solid foundation part. And we've all seen or heard of much stranger gifts from husbands than that one.

Like Meg, 45, whose 40th birthday came along in the fifth year of her marriage: "A battle was roaring at our house over checking the air in the car tires. He said that I should do it since I drove the car more often. I said it was his responsibility since the car was in his name. To get his point across, he asked all my birthday guests to give me a tire gauge for my present. I received *fifteen!*"

At least these men both possess a sense of humor, however twisted it might be. Karen from Kentucky was preparing to turn 40. When her husband asked her what she wanted, "I told him that I'd love to change places with him for one day so I could see how fun I've been to live with for seventeen years. (He didn't laugh either)."

When you marry a little later in life, strange gifts are just the tip of the adjustment iceberg. Our first Sunday as a married couple, we walked through the door of our honeymoon cottage after church, Bill flopped down on the couch, snapped open the Sunday paper, and asked, "What's for dinner?"

My stomach sank to my knees. My Playtex Living Gloves were on their deathbed at the very idea. It wasn't the work I resented. It was the automatic expectations and feeling taken for granted. Besides, I'm a mediocre cook at best. Like my humorist friend Susan Vass says, "When my kids see me getting near the stove, they yell out, 'Hot! Hot!'"

After several months of eating my "gourmet" meals (i.e., dish after dish of "blackened" food), Bill decided to try his hand at cooking. First, it was muffins for a Saturday morning treat, then Tuesdays became Dad's night to cook. Soon, we added Thursday evenings to the agenda. When a friend gave him a chef's hat for Christmas one year, the transition became official: Bill is the designated cook of the family. Applause, please.

Now, the obvious concern is that I'll take him for granted in his role as the breadmaker of the family. I'll admit, I've sung out, "What's for dinner?" more than once. When Bill says, "I've cooked the last eleven meals," I realize that if he's adding it up that carefully the thrill is gone, and it's my turn to cook.

In our marriage, we've divided domestic duties based on skills and willingness, trying to avoid stereotypes and expectations.

And burnt offerings for dinner.

Here's an accidental, all-too-common problem that years of marriage can produce. My friend Dolley and her hubby gave each other the kind of 40th birthday party they hoped to have themselves. She's outgoing, he's mellow. She gave him a huge surprise party (mistake), then he gave her a quiet weekend away, just for two (oops). She admits, "We got our signals crossed!"

Paint this signal red: Ocilla shares, "When I turned 40, my husband began introducing me to his friends as his grandmother. After a year, I began introducing him as my first husband!"

Then there's Bonnie's discovery: "You look at your husband and think, 'My, he looks like a man in his 60s!' Then suddenly remember that you're a few months older than he is."

In our tenth year of marriage, Bill and I wrote an article together called "Seven Ways to Tear Down (or Build Up) Your Mate." *Do not try this at home.*

"Bill," I said, as my hands hovered over the computer keyboard, "why don't you come up with a list of seven ways we unintentionally tear each other down? I'll do the same, and then we'll compare notes."

"Fine," he said, dropping into the chair beside my desk. "I've been thinking about the time we were driving to my parents' house."

"Nah, that'll never work," I said with conviction, my eyes still glued to the computer screen. "Too negative."

"No, I mean that time over Christmas when the kids . . ."

"I remember what happened!" I said, exasperated. "Your mom made some comment about Matthew's grades and . . ."

"Not that time, Liz."

"And then I said she didn't understand the situation and then she said . . ."

"Please let me finish!" Bill's volume control had moved up three full notches.

"Finish what?" I asked innocently.

He jumped to his feet. "*That* will be the first thing on my list!"

"What list?" My dancing fingers paused over the keyboard.

"The list of the seven ways we tear each other down. 'Not letting me finish a sentence' will be number one!"

"Do I do that?" My expression was pure Shirley Temple.

"Oh, brother!" Bill rolled his eyes toward the heavens. "Honey, sometimes you're so sure of what I'm going to say next, you say it for me, even if that's not the direction I'm headed at all."

"Oh. Sorry." Sheepish grin. "I'll try to do better. Now . . . what were you saying?"

I recently stumbled upon a horrible verse in Proverbs: "Better to dwell in a corner of a housetop, / Than in a house shared with a contentious woman." Oh, Lord, is that a hint? Even worse, the identical verse shows up twice, in Proverbs 21:9 *and* Proverbs 25:24! Solomon obviously had an ax to grind. Or, he was talking about two different wives (after all, he had several hundred).

Say! Maybe the second time he meant to substitute the words "contentious *teenager*" for "contentious wife." Maybe.

The Good News Is . . .

After a decade of togetherness, Bill and I have learned that the best way to affirm each other is to *listen:* Eyes open, ears open, heart open, mouth shut. Occasional nodding helps, too.

Such low-impact exercises are perfect for the over-40 couple. They conserve energy, save wear and tear on the marriage, and allow your man to follow the proverbial command to "rejoice with the wife of your youth."[13] Youth? Better hurry, Bill.

My dear husband took me to a lodge, rented a suite for the night with a hot tub in the room, ordered my favorite pizza, and rented my favorite movie. He forgot one small detail: a baby-sitter! We spent my 40th birthday swimming in the hot tub with children (4 and 5 year olds), watching the kids' favorite movie, *The Lion King*. It was just wonderful! I wouldn't change a thing.

Cathy from Ohio, 40

REASON 15

Name badges
are no longer
tacky. They're
necessary.

NAME BADGES ARE NO LONGER TACKY.
THEY'RE NECESSARY.

I developed a new skill after 40: name-dropping. I don't mean slipping a few celebrity names into my conversation, I mean looking at someone I've known for ten years and not being able to even remember the first letter of their name.

For years we shunned ugly paper "Hello, My Name Is" tags with curly edges, or heavy name badges that poked nasty holes in our best silk blouses. *How silly!* we'd think smugly. *Who needs name tags? I know every person at this conference, plus the names of their spouses, kids, and pet chameleon. Name badges are for old people.*

The first time your tongue gets stuck to the roof of your long-term memory, your opinion of name tags begins to shift.

Now our bifocaled eyes light up at computer-generated tags done in a big, bold 36-point font. "Hi, Joan," we confidently shout across the room. "Haven't seen you in years!" *Whew.*

Lately I've been wishing that all the mothers at school would embroider their names on their collars. Or, just wear the same clothes every time I see them, to keep the Jennys and the Judys straight. Even a big sweater with a "J" on it would be helpful.

Actually, if I could talk the whole east end of town into permanent name tags, that would take care of my fading memory problem nicely.

Lucky for me, name tags are usually *de rigueur* at the conferences and retreats where I'm the speaker. People often don't remember they have them on, though. I'll reach for a book to sign and say, "Is this for you, Karen?"

The color drains from her face. *How did she know?* she wonders.

I think I'm pretty clever, until I accidentally leave my own name tag on and stop by the grocery store on the way home.

"Hello, Liz Curtis Higgs!" the clerk sings out.

I smile with simpering modesty. "Oh, you read my books?"

"No, I read your name tag."

After an experience at the Dallas airport, I'll never leave a name tag on again. A woman saw me sitting there and said excitedly, "Oh! Where did you just see Liz Curtis Higgs? I heard her years ago and she was so funny!"

"Um . . . I *am* Liz Curtis Higgs," I responded, not sure whether to be offended or amused.

Her face turned ashen and she started to stammer. "Y-y-you can't be Liz! I would never have recognized you!"

Uh-oh. What does that mean??

She quickly buried her head in a book, never to look up again. Which means she probably missed when I carefully slipped off my name tag and deposited it into the nearest trash can. Dangerous for the self-esteem, these little tags.

Jeanne from California declares, "With my memory failing me so badly, I've taken to wildly gesturing to try to make myself understood. My head knows what I want to say but my mouth refuses to spit it out! I feel as if I'm caught up in an eternal game of charades."

My advice? When you stumble over something you not only didn't forget, you never *knew*, plead "poor memory" and start making stuff up.

My sister Sarah, twelve years my senior and therefore farther along the memory-loss trail, joined me for a shopping excursion at a lovely craft-and-basket place in New Jersey. Soon after we stepped inside, she saw a tempting display of yummy-looking imported chocolates wrapped in foil. Sarah scooped two up for our dessert later, and proceeded to walk all through the store with these little bonbons in her hand.

Her nice, warm hand.

When we finally got to the checkout counter an hour later, baskets and silk flowers hanging all over us, Sarah opened her fingers and looked at the brown gooey mess with shock. *What is this?*

The clerk behind the register was aghast. "May I help you?"

Sarah turned beet red and said sheepishly, "We have a little problem here."

The woman handed us a roll of paper towels and turned away in disgust. I was no help at all, since I was laughing so hard I couldn't breathe let alone form the word *Chocolate!* that would've put the clerk out of her misery.

If Matthew and Lillian had been with us, it never would've happened. Kids have incredible memories. Oh, not about important items like lunch money or homework, but memorizing two thousand intricate moves on a Nintendo game? No sweat.

One of Matthew's computer games is called *Rememory.* The concept is simple: Find two matching icons on a board of twenty-six different pairs. Look at two, turn them back over. Like *The Match Game* without the questions.

The first time through *Rememory,* my mind was a steel trap, matching icons with joy and abandon. But the second time through, my brain was a leaky tin can, still hanging on to bits and pieces of the first game. *Wasn't that green diamond-shaped thing over in this corner? What? An orange triangle? Oh dear.* In the game of *Rememory,* I can only play once.

Bill is the serious computer geek at our house, though when I called him that once he turned his sea-colored eyes on me and said, "That's *Dr.* Geek to you!" Watching me struggle with an uncooperative computer software package recently, he sighed and said, "I guess I'm going to have to break down and buy you some more memory, Liz."

Oh, if only he could.

The Good News Is . . .

Bill assures me that computers are *not* smarter than we are, they just do incredibly simple things at incredibly high speeds. Like remembering someone's name, for instance. Now with my handy database at my fingertips, my memory has discovered the fountain of youth.

An old client from 1991 calls? No problem, I'll search for her name by year, month, even day.

Someone heard me speak in Topeka? Got 'em, in thirty seconds.

You're a fellow writer? No, you're in the "W" category.

Can't remember how to spell your name? Relax, I'll put it in the "sounds like" mode!

With a zip-plus-four code to remember, tons of new area codes, and our four family social security stats to keep straight, I went with something very safe for my on-line handle. All I have to do is look at my name badge: LizHiggs@aol.com. Even I can remember that.

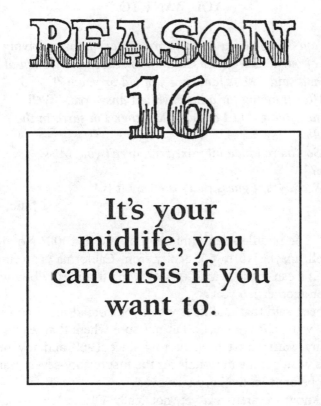

REASON 16

It's your
midlife, you
can crisis if you
want to.

IT'S YOUR MIDLIFE, YOU CAN CRISIS IF
YOU WANT TO.

I am a director at a child care center and was driving
one of our kindergarten children to school. He looked at
me and said, "Miss Jane, are you old or young?"
*   After thinking for a little while I answered, "Well,*
I'm not young, but I am not old either. I'm sorta in the
middle."
*   "So you're kinda all mixed up, aren't you, Miss*
Jane?"
*   "Well, yes, I guess that's the way it is."*

Jane, 43

The Middle Ages. Hmmm. A.D. 500 to 1500? No, 40 to
60. Well, maybe 45 to 65. Scotty from California is "trying to
decide if I can make it to 100, so I won't technically be middle
aged for another ten years."

It's been said that midlife is when your broad mind and your
narrow waist change places. I'm not sure where that leaves me,
since my waist hasn't been narrow since 1968 and my broad
mind is what got me in trouble for the first twenty-seven years of
my life before I let the Lord take over!

We know we aren't *old* yet, not really. Old is Methuselah, a
man who spent 969 years on this earth, then poof. *He* didn't hit
midlife until his 485th birthday.

Forty is *far* from being old. In fact, it's the same distance from
being young. Young is two hours of sleep and no makeup. Old is
also two hours of sleep and no makeup. Forty is smack in the
middle: eight hours of sleep and tons of makeup.

Before the decade is out, we'll be right where Julia from
Colorado sees us: "Too old for Tampax and Midol, too young for

Attends and Medicare." Donna, 43, loves this middle ground of life: "No matter what you say or do, it can be explained away, 'I'm in midlife crisis!'"

I'm not in crisis, I'm in denial. On those mornings when I creak out of bed and shuffle down the hall, I keep telling myself, "Relax, Liz. Any day now, you'll feel as good as ever. This has just been a stressful week."

The 40s are a bit like our 20s were, an awkward time of social adjustment, trying to figure out where we "fit" in the grand scheme of things. In our teens, we're busy making friends. In our 20s, we're making our move up the ladder of career success. In our 30s, we're making money and, perhaps, a name for ourselves. Then, in our 40s, we're trying to make sense of it all, especially if we haven't amassed the fame, fortune, or friends we'd hoped for.

At 40, life not only pulls the rug out from under us, it knocks out two walls and puts in a skylight. The world doesn't look right anymore. We say things like, "Is it my imagination, or is the HR department hiring them younger every year?" Cindy, 43, finds it difficult "trying to get into a university physician assistant program when you're competing with 20 year olds who can 'boot up' computers to do chemistry equations and I'm still using a slide rule." Suzanne commiserates: "It's tough being interviewed by a young 20-something who is making the hiring decisions when you have salt-and-pepper hair, a few extra pounds, and age spots."

The people we always looked up to—physicians, airline pilots, professors, those older role models, those paragons of maturity—suddenly look too young to be in charge. Linda, 48, says, "Policemen look much younger, like not old enough to drive let alone give you a ticket." And Jeanne has a hard time "accepting the young baby-face doctor examining me!" Patt, 47, agrees that she'd like to "see some ID before I remove any clothing."

Even worse, these young whippersnappers (I've always wanted to use that word) seem to be doing better than we are. Driving through a high-ticket subdivision, I mutter to myself, "How can someone who's only 35 afford a house like that?"

Easy: At 25, I went to parties. They went to med school.

I find myself sitting on planes next to women with nicer clothes, fancier laptop computers, better jewelry, and then realize they are fifteen years younger than I.

Oh help, Lord! Is this how it's going to be?

Yes and no. Yes, our coworkers and caretakers are getting younger every year. No, we don't have to get depressed about it.

Debi, 41, is enjoying herself too much to worry about her age. "I sang karaoke for the first time and didn't care what I sounded like. If it takes turning 40 to have that much fun, then it's worth it!"

Rebecca, meanwhile, is having a good time being in charge: "When I turned 40, I ran for public office and won. The confidence and vision seemed to converge at 40."

Confidence. That word kept popping up in the stories women sent me. I think it's a combination of experience—the kind that only forty-plus years on the planet can give you—plus that "pressure is off" freedom, seasoned with wisdom and greater financial resources.

Or, it could be hormones.

When Ruth turned 41, she wanted to learn a new skill. "I like a challenge and motorcycling is it!" She owns a nice royal blue Honda Rebel 250cc and a white helmet with the words "Hot Flash" written on it. Her next challenge? "Getting in shape for a hiking and boating trip down the Amazon." What a woman.

Buni from Ohio takes the prize—literally:

I've raced high-performance Corvette race cars for a number of years. Once I set my helmet down near the registration desk to fill out some papers and walked away from it. A few hours later, when I came up to retrieve it, the new young man behind the desk handed it to me saying, "Oh, yes ma'am, here is your son's helmet."

I smiled, noted the name Buni on the side, and informed him it was mine.

He said, "But you're old enough to be my mom!"
"No, I'm old enough to be your grandmom."
As I walked away, a more experienced driver standing there informed him that I was a nine-time national champion driver. I heard the young man exclaim, "Good grief, I thought you had to retire long before then!"

Buni, 51

The Good News Is . . .

Buni is not planning on having a midlife crisis anytime soon.

I got a birthday cake decorated with an ugly man in a bikini swimsuit, dead roses, and a basket filled with tasteless gifts for older folks including a cookbook called, "Cooking in the Nude." The third-grade class made me old age cards. The fourth grade cried into their Kleenex when they saw me. An announcement was made over the loud speaker in memory of my youth. And when I left school, the sign in front of my car said "Parking for the elderly only." All this from a group of usually kind elementary teachers.

Sarah from Alabama, 50

REASON 17

Your kids are old enough to handle their own late-night feedings.

YOUR KIDS ARE OLD ENOUGH TO HANDLE THEIR OWN LATE-NIGHT FEEDINGS.

If you got married when you were supposed to—at age 21—and gave birth to your firstborn when you were expected to—at age 24—then you have a special treat waiting for you when you turn 40: a teenager with a driver's license.

The prophet Jeremiah described the scene well:

> *They are silly children,*
> *And they have no understanding.*
> *They are wise to do evil,*
> *But to do good they have no knowledge.*[14]

Donna awoke on her 40th birthday "to find that my daughter and her boyfriend had stretched a huge banner across the entire front lawn, which read 'Happy 40th Birthday, Mom, we love you!' I almost died. I've managed to keep my age from the neighbors for all these years, now everyone knows how old I really am!"

With teenagers under your roof, "there's never a dull moment in this house," says Margaret, 46. "I'd like one though (just one)."

I'll be 47 before I have a teenager in the house. My daughter will be scaling the heights of hysterical puberty when I am wallowing in the valley of menopause. Please mark your calendar, so you don't accidentally call me during any of those years.

Jane, 43, is grappling with "having teenage daughters and being told they are lovely young women. Gulp! Am I old enough to have women as daughters?" (Yes, Jane. We're all old enough, whether we have daughters or not.) Another Jane has had "several people ask me if I am my daughter's *sister*. I love it but she doesn't. Of course, they do preface the question with *older* sister!"

At any age, some kids make your hair stand on end. For Vicki, 46, her teenagers changed her hairstyle completely. "You revert to wearing bangs to hide the frown lines caused by the looks you gave your children when they misbehaved. We used to take naps with our children to get them to rest; now we take naps so that we can wait up for our teenagers when they have a long evening out!"

I'm hoping that if I retain my slightly askew personality all through my 40s, my kids will automatically go the opposite direction in rebellion and turn out okay.

Jeanne gets a kick out of "watching my daughter do all the things she used to criticize me for and now doesn't think are so bad after all." She's also amused "when my son shares his recipes with me. Who does he think cooked for him all those years he was growing up?"

Carol, 51, has a hard time "convincing my kids I understand their problems, that once, long ago, I had the same experiences." Julia, 42, agrees that no matter what we say to them, "teenagers won't ever believe that you were once their age!"

I've dragged out old scrapbooks to prove to my children, beyond a shadow of a doubt, that I was once a child, even younger than they are now. They giggle, but I'm not sure they get it.

"Mom, why are you lifting your dress up over your head in this picture?" Lillian squeals.

I assure her that she did the same thing when *she* was 4, but she refuses to believe me. Even *I'm* not crazy enough to show them my teenage photos, though. I was a bona fide, small-town hippie freak. Torn jeans, tie-dyed shirt, and clogs. In other words, I was right in style and would be again if that stuff still fit.

Maybe not. There's nothing worse than seeing a mature woman trying to look like a teenager. Susan from Indiana is facing "the realization that I am in no way 'hip, cool, bad, or radical' in the eyes of our teenage baby-sitter and her friends. My list of adjectives, no doubt, further proves my point."

Lori's 14-year-old daughter is so determined to keep her 40-year-old mother dressed in cool threads that she takes her shopping. Why? So she can wear her mother's clothes. Devious.

Having teenage daughters means dating, then weddings, even grandchildren may loom on the not-so-distant horizon. This is the part I dread most a decade from now: seeing every boyfriend as a potential husband for Lillian. Oh dear.

One woman at a presentation told me that her daughter is dating a man who is 23 and has an imaginary friend. The mother encouraged her by saying, "Well, that's a perfectly normal childhood fantasy," to which the daughter replied, "Yeah, but he just met him two months ago."

The Good News Is . . .

There *are* women who have survived mothering teenagers. See that blonde in the next pew over, the one with laugh lines that converge into crow's-feet? She made it. Or, how about your friend from work who just came dancing home from her daughter's college graduation? That sigh of relief says it all: You can send a child through college and live to tell about it.

Janice from Connecticut is "amazed at what caring, intelligent, sensitive, and loving people they are, now producing their own offspring. I am so lucky!"

How like us women to give "luck" the credit for all our hard work! Mikki from California is thrilled with how her efforts have paid off: "My children are wonderful, loving adults. I am closing the door on raising them and throwing open the door to my *new* life, exploring my options, expanding my horizons, and pushing beyond my comfort levels. What fun!"

And *fun* is what life after 40 is all about.

REASON

18

Millions of
women give
birth after 40.
(Is this the
"fun" part?)

MILLIONS OF WOMEN GIVE BIRTH AFTER 40.
(IS THIS THE "FUN" PART?)

We've considered the implications of mothering teenagers while turning 40, but what of the woman who is still adding to the family tree at 40 and beyond?

I was born in my mother's 43rd year. I was a surprise. A shock. A disaster, even. She'd already mothered five children, one right after another. Then, after enjoying nine long years of peace from pregnancy, it was back to maternity clothes for Mom. She was mortified. None of her Garden Club friends were having babies in their 40s, for heaven's sake.

After I arrived on the scene Mom had to fit in her gardening whenever she could, often at odd hours. One starlit summer night I called out the back door looking for her. "Mom! M-o-m-m-m!" No sound, no movement. Had she stumbled in the asparagus patch? Was she lost among the sunflowers?

Finally I got a flashlight and bravely ventured out into the spooky garden filled with shadows that didn't resemble my mother at all. After several frantic minutes of searching I discovered her on the far edge of our property, precariously balanced on a steep embankment, planting marigolds by the light of the moon.

At least I always knew where to find her. Arriving home from school each day, I'd find her bent over her poppies or plucking petunias. That round, blue-jeaned bottom pointing skyward was a very comforting sight. Years later, when I passed a garden center displaying a decorative plywood figure of a bent-over woman in polka-dot pantaloons, I cried out in astonishment, "That's my mother!"

Makes me wonder how my own children will remember me. I'm usually bending over a computer keyboard, not a garden patch, so my big, round bottom is parked in a chair, not pointing in the air. Thank goodness for that.

My guess is they will remember me by sound more than sight. Specifically, the sound of their mother whining: "Who left the milk out again?" or "What year did we last change the litter box?" or "Why can't these pillows stay on the couch?" (Because they are *throw* pillows, of course. The children are just trying to follow orders.)

Matthew and Lillian think I'm ancient, born when television was new, only came in black and white, and didn't have video games growing out of the sets like tentacles. Linda, 42, has a hard time "convincing my children I didn't live with the dinosaurs." Karen from Indiana remembers pushing her preschooler through a crowded store in a shopping cart. "My daughter asked me very sincerely, but a little too loudly, 'I forget, Mommy, are you 83 or 38?'"

Children can be so entertaining.

> *While shopping one day I met a high school friend I hadn't seen since graduation. My 8-year-old son was with me and her 18-year-old daughter was with her. After we talked and then went our separate ways, my son asked, "If you went to school together, why is she old enough to have a teenager and you only have me?"*
>
> **Nancy, 41**

That's what happens when you teach higher math to third graders.

There was a time when your peer group included women who were not only your age, but had children the same ages as yours. No more. These days, a 40-year-old mother-to-be may attend Lamaze class with women ten or *twenty* years younger. Sure, we can give birth after 40, but will we have the energy to chase them around at 43?

I can hear the angst in Roxanne's words when she writes, "I have just turned 41 and have a 4 year old and a 17 month old and I'm 'giving' all the time. I'm where my mother was at 24." Contrast that with Dorothy's experience: "By my 40th birthday, the kids were in school and I was healthier, happier, and 'younger'!"

I don't know about you, but when a 20-something woman asks me, "Should I have kids first, or work on my career now and have kids later?" I respond with gusto: "Have your children while you're young!" A mature mother may have more wisdom and patience, but she also has more aches and pains. The truth is, we don't usually get to choose if or when our mothering will begin. When children arrive, rejoice and remember to take frequent naps.

Scotty is having her first at 40 and is thrilled to pieces: "I figure, as my daughter's growing up I'll be in my second childhood! Plus, when I'm 70 and need help in my golden years, she'll be too young to refuse!" Posy from Connecticut is counting on that, too, since after fourteen years of marriage, she became a mother at 40 and "found out forty-eight hours later that all my answers to 'How to Parent' went down the drain!"

Beverley found out that being 40 and pregnant is downright newsworthy:

> *Our family had just moved into a new home. I was inside putting things away, frustrated because I was moving so slowly. My husband, being the outgoing, lovable soul he is, was outside introducing himself and our children to the neighbors. When they asked about his wife, he didn't even tell them my name as he smiled his biggest smile, beamed with pride, and said, (as if it was some kind of miracle), "She's 40 and eight months pregnant!"*

The Good News Is . . .

A baby at any age is a blessing.

I was a newlywed of eight months, wrestling with a big, fat turkey, when impending motherhood knocked on my door. I was too preoccupied with getting my first Thanksgiving dinner on the table to even notice all the telltale symptoms.

It was almost 2:00—Zero Hour—when Bill's family was scheduled to arrive. I was running around like a crazy woman, fussing at Bill for not being more helpful. "Celebrating Thanksgiving at our house was your idea, remember? Your idea, your family, and you didn't even help! This is the last time I try and impress that bunch, believe me!" Suddenly I froze. Someone was gently knocking on the glass of our front door, just a few feet away.

Realization and dread poured over me like gravy on mashed potatoes. Handing Bill the vacuum, I opened the front door with a sickly grin and faced the inevitable. "Hi, folks," I said faintly, swallowing hard. "Happy Thanksgiving."

"Really?" my mother-in-law said, raising an eyebrow as she walked past me, casserole in hand.

"Sorry you caught me having a hissy fit," I continued, with a weary sigh. "It's been a challenging day." *Why was I so tired and cranky?* I wondered.

We had plenty of time to smooth things over, since the turkey didn't come out of the oven until nearly six o'clock. I, however, couldn't eat a bite. Couldn't even bear the smell of it. For a woman who loves to eat as much as I do, this was a rare moment indeed. "Not even a slice of my delicious chocolate pie?" Nanny asked, and I felt my stomach flip over.

Just what I need, I thought, *some intestinal flu thing for the long holiday weekend ahead.* Exhausted, I excused myself to stretch out on the couch while dear Bill handled kitchen duty. Not long after, his family murmured their good-byes as I offered a wimpy wave from my prone position in the living room.

"Honey, are you okay?" Bill asked, kneeling beside the sofa and looking intently at my chalk-white face.

"I'll be all right," I mumbled, but even I was not convinced. By Saturday morning, the queasiness had settled in to stay, even after plenty of sleep, no cooking, a quiet house, and a day off work.

Well, there *was* one other possible explanation, outrageous as it seemed. After a quick trip to the drugstore that morning, I spent a little extra time in the rest room with a home pregnancy test, feeling like a chemist and shaking like a leaf.

Minutes later, Bill and I sat at the kitchen table and watched with fear and excitement as the little vial changed color, and the truth changed our lives forever. It was neither romantic nor touching, but it is what I said: "It's a go, Higgs!"

We were indeed with child.

Two old people, latecomers to marriage, wed to our careers, strangers to parenting, thrilled to the tips of our toes. Happy Birth-day, indeed.

On my 40th birthday, I was eight months pregnant. My sister had secretly arranged for a balloon-bearing, telegram-singing gorilla to show up at our house—even my husband didn't know about it. I screamed when the gorilla walked into the family room, which made my 20 month old cry and my husband come running. I made a comment about going into early labor, which must have rattled the gorilla because he cut his visit short. Then my sister was upset because she didn't think she got her money's worth. She turns 40 this year. Revenge will be sweet!

Patsy from South Dakota, 41

REASON
19

Home decor
moves beyond
wedding
presents and
kid-proof
slipcovers.

HOME DECOR MOVES BEYOND WEDDING PRESENTS AND KID-PROOF SLIPCOVERS.

Here's a *big* plus about life after 40: You can buy a decent couch—ivory or beige this time, if you like—without the burden of considering, "How will this look with grape juice or graham crackers ground into it?" (Unless, of course, you had a post-40 baby, in which case, hang in there, that light-colored sofa is in your future, too.) Want a glass-top table? Now that tiny hands have grown bigger and are driving cars and pushing keyboard buttons, a clear glass table is yours, with a free bottle of Windex. Look, Mom, no fingerprints!

Best of all, you get your knickknacks back. All those glass doohickeys and ceramic thingamabobs that you hid way up on the top bookshelf for years, safe from preschool pulverizing, can return to roost on your coffee table once again.

Of course, there are some items you were relieved to have tucked away that may never see the light of day again. Some of them—a plastic pink flamingo yard ornament, an "antique" wire rug beater with the Woolworth's tag still attached—were purchased at yard sales in a weak moment. Others crept into our lives on the coattails of men we promised to love, honor, and obey, even if their apartments were decorated in early Boy Scout camp when we met them.

A mail-order company asked a sampling of brides: "What was the most challenging decorating item your new husband contributed to your married life?" Their answers will hardly surprise those of us who've been shoving boxes marked "His Stuff" around the attic for years.

"Deer Antlers" was first on the list of undesirables. How well we know. We hide them in family rooms and basements, spare bedrooms and out-of-the-way workshops. One woman I know bought a cabin in the mountains with the express purpose of having somewhere to stash her husband's collection of heads and horns. Real estate is a very expensive solution, but you must admit, it's clever. For those of us with tighter budgets, a carefully chosen spot in the garage will have to suffice.

"Stuffed Fish" also appeared in the difficult-to-decorate-around department. A mounted rainbow trout wouldn't be so bad, but when they bring home a marlin, taste goes out the window. A seven-foot fish simply isn't flat enough to turn into a coffee table, and besides, the two-foot fin would wreak havoc on your panty hose every time you walked through the room.

"Potbellied Stoves" were a common complaint among many new brides, although no one I know has confessed to inheriting such an item on their wedding day. A husband with a potbelly, perhaps, but no stove!

"Weights" were next on the list, to which many of us would say, "Amen!" An educated guess would put the majority of those barbells in the far corner of the bedroom closet where they periodically roll around and squish the toes of our favorite dress shoes. Since I have a five-pound pair of my own hand weights in that pile, I won't throw the first stone at this decorative transgression.

And what did the brides say was the toughest addition to their furniture families? "Moose Heads." You can almost hear Alaskan wives groaning with understanding. Women who moved north to the forty-ninth state in search of a husband, only to discover the sobering truth: The odds are good, but the goods are odd.

A woman in Milwaukee got a fowl-feathered friend when she tied the knot. It seems her husband grew up in a small town with a butcher shop that displayed a six-foot neon chicken in the window. When they went out of business, hubby bought the neon nightmare.

"Where is it now?" I asked her.

"In our dining room," she replied. "And when we have chicken, we turn it on!"

To be sure, there are men with a highly developed sense of home decorating, but sometimes their style leaves our taste buds cold. Suppose he wants an ultramodern, glass-encased living space and she's into country cute and quilts on the wall. Will she toss fringed coverlets on his Danish-modern sofa? Will he arrange her collection of cast-iron roosters in an abstract geometric pattern on the deck? Can this marriage be saved?

At our house, the wedding of our decorating styles was made easier because my husband, Bill, has no taste whatsoever. I don't mean he's a bohemian, I mean he has the exact same response to every item on the furniture showroom floor: "That's fine."

His lack of discernment in this arena revealed itself early in our relationship. The first time I visited his apartment I held my breath as he opened the door. Would it be early trading stamps? Late Salvation Army?

It was plaid. Inexpensive plaid. Very inexpensive.

Fairly tidy, though, and that earned several points. Little did I know that in preparing for my visit, it took Bill several days to even find the floor.

Wisely, he kept the real showstopper among his collectibles out of sight on that first visit. Bill, you see, went to college for twelve years—full-time—to earn that Ph.D. in Hebrew. That meant his loved ones had twelve long years to save up and buy the perfect graduation gift for this godly young man. They bought him a Last Supper Talking Clock.

Words can hardly describe it, but I'll try. It's big: thirty-two inches long, twenty inches tall. It features that famous painting of the Last Supper (the one where they're all on the same side of the table) on velvet. In front of each one of the apostles there's a little plastic candle. At the top of the hour, every hour, one of the candles lights up, and from deep within the clock comes a voice: "It's eight o'clock, and I am John. Bong!"

And that's not all. Then you hear soft music, eight chimes, and a verse of Scripture. The thing goes on for four minutes. It's also battery operated, so there's no unsightly cord hanging down. How tasteful. And, it's voice activated. Not only does this clock talk to you, but if you wanted to—on a slow day—you could talk to it. If you don't hear well, no problem, because there's a big display of the time in glowing red numerals, right up front between the bread and the wine.

When Bill and I got engaged, it was time for me to meet The Clock. I took one look at it and said what any self-respecting woman would say: "Yard Sale!" Bill's face was crestfallen. His graduation gift, of all things. A receipt was left in the box in case we ever had to get it worked on, which revealed the unbelievable, undeniable truth: Those generous souls had paid $1,400 for this collector's item.

We were stuck with it.

Since I was the home owner when Bill and I married, I thought I ought to at least get a vote about where the clock went. I suggested the back porch. (We don't have one.)

First, we tried putting it in the family room, right over the couch. It didn't look too bad, and it certainly was a conversation piece (in more ways than one). Problem was, Bill was accustomed to this clock, and I was not. So, every time one of the disciples started talking in the other room, I yelled out, "Who is it?"

"Andrew!" the clock boomed back.

Then we tried just hanging it up when one of the gift-givers dropped by for a visit. I found out it's pretty hard to hang a three-foot clock while the doorbell is ringing.

Finally my decorating dignity reigned and into the hall closet it went. We tipped the clock on its side, carefully slid it in between the coats, and forgot all about it. Until one night when we had company over for dinner. One of my friends was standing in close proximity to the closet and said, tapping his watch, "What time is it, anyway?"

From back behind the coats, a muffled voice declared: "It's 7:15, and I am Peter. Bong!"

The Good News Is . . .

The next time you sigh with discouragement as you watch your husband dance through the door with yet another bowling trophy for your china cupboard, or a stuffed quail for the mantel, or a fresh set of antlers for the foyer, take solace in this thought: *At least they're quiet.*

REASON 20

Statistically,
you're less
likely to spend
time in a
penitentiary.

STATISTICALLY, YOU'RE LESS LIKELY TO SPEND TIME IN A PENITENTIARY.

Every single day of this decade, twelve thousand U.S. citizens are turning 40. I *thought* I heard America screaming.
But the statistics are really in our favor here:

1. You were one of the lucky ones who made it to 40.
2. You will never have to turn 40 again, ever.

Deb, 47, from Pennsylvania, thinks, "the best thing about being over 40 is not having to anticipate it anymore. I've reached that generic age where there is no obvious group into which I fall. Everyone is my peer except for the very young or the very old. I do not in any way feel 'chronologically challenged'!"

I'm beginning to worry about finishing all of the craft kits I bought.

Forty is a number that shouldn't worry us for a minute since, statistically speaking, women live longer than men. Even so, we're never going to get everything done. Beverly from Colorado struggles with "knowing that I have so much to finish in my life. Can't possibly get it all done, so will have to make priorities and stick to them."

This whole crazy book jumped into my head when my friend Susan sent me one man's list of "Seven Reasons to Look Forward to Age 40," based on statistical and empirical evidence. Here are some of the points this gentleman made, with my own interpretations:

1. You'll be safe from the draft, even in wartime.

Fella, women *are* safe from the draft.

2. Thanks to immunities, you'll have fewer colds.

That's not immunities, that's because our kids are are no longer dragging germs home from kindergarten.

3. You'll have far less chance of being maimed in an auto accident, struck by a bullet, or hurt in a swimming-pool mishap.

Oh, I can explain those, too. Auto accident? Over-40s always wear seat belts, ever since we saw that awful film in Driver's Ed with the guy who fell out his door and got crushed by a tree.

Struck by a bullet? We no longer date men who carry guns.

And the pool mishap is obvious: Most of us haven't gone near the edge of a swimming pool in fifteen years.

4. You'll be at less risk of developing mental instability.

What a relief, since one of the symptoms of menopause is *thinking* you are mentally unstable.

5. Your life expectancy will be about sixteen months greater than it was when you were 20.

I may not be terrific at math, but I think we have a serious error in calculation here. My life expectancy at 20 was probably sixty more years, and now it's only forty more years. This does not sound like a "greater than" situation, this sounds like a "less than." What's sixteen more months when we're talking about an overall loss of twenty years? Still, you have to applaud that kind of proactive thinking. When I hit 80, I promise to throw a "Sixteen More Months!" party in his honor.

6. You'll suffer a little less stomach pain, dental pain, muscle pain, headache, and backache than a typical 20 year old does.

What kind of "typical" 20 year old are we talking about? If the kind he has in mind parties till dawn, drinks cheap wine, breakdances on the pavement, and hasn't seen a dentist since he was 12, well, yes. We do take better care of ourselves than that.

7. You'll be much less likely to spend time in a penitentiary.

Of course, this only follows. If you're not avoiding the draft, sneezing on policemen, dodging bullets, becoming mentally unglued, partying until you drop, or living as if it's your last day on earth, you probably won't even know where the local penitentiary is located.

The Good News Is . . .

Statistics indicate that people who laugh at least fifteen times a day live longer than people who fret about everything, including statistics. By counting your giggles instead of your wrinkles, by giving worry the boot in favor of a "hoot," your *laugh* expectancy is guaranteed to increase 100 percent!

I asked my husband to keep my 40th birthday very low key. Our crew, a group of four couples who have shared everything, decided low key was not to be. When Larry and I returned to our home later that evening, every piece of furniture in the living room was gone and all our bedroom furniture was there plus a few tasteless additions, like an ugly statue, six or seven feet tall, wearing my "nightie." The contents of the vacuum cleaner were dumped out, giving the impression I was not a tidy housekeeper. The pillows on our bed were heavily perfumed with an awful fragrance. When we heard giggling going on outside, we discovered our patio tastefully decorated with our living room furniture, birthday cake, decorations, and a crowd of friends enjoying every painful expression I had on my face.

Carolyn from California, 61

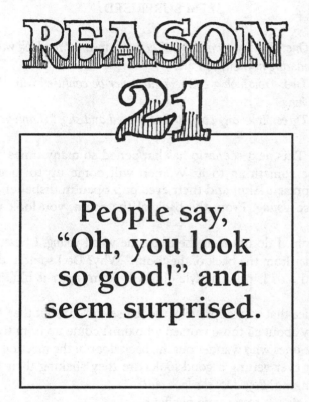

REASON 21

People say, "Oh, you look so good!" and seem surprised.

PEOPLE SAY, "OH, YOU LOOK SO GOOD!" AND SEEM SURPRISED.

Rule One: *"You look wonderful!" actually means "You look wonderful, considering how old you are."*
Rule Two: *"You look great!" should never be confused with "You're great looking."*
Rule Three: *Take any compliment offered and say, "Thank you!"*

This next scenario has happened so many times, there must be something to it: Women will come up to meet me after a presentation and their eyes pop open in disbelief. "Oh, you're so *young!* From the back of the room, you look much older."

Hmmm. I do not hear them say the word *young,* I hear, "You look *older* from the back of the room." Why? Do I stand old? Am I shaped old? Is my hairstyle old? Maybe my *voice* is old, is that it?

It's nice that they approve of the "close-up" Liz, but then I start to worry about all those women who don't come up front to greet me. The ones who wander out the back door of the meeting room without ever getting a good look. Are they shaking their heads and thinking, *Boy, does she look old?*

Oh, this *is* a sorry state of affairs.

Maybe I should slip out a side door right after I speak ("Elvis has left the building"), so I can be waiting for them big as life when the back doors open. Ta-da! Younger than springtime, here I am.

My friend humorist Hope Mihalap, 61, recently showed up at a speakers convention sporting a knockout wardrobe. I oohed and aahed over her snazzy new duds until she finally made this confession:

When you get well past 40, you do a dangerous thing: You run out and buy more expensive and glamorous clothes than you really need. And I think I know why: You harbor the confused and mistaken idea that these elegant clothes will make you look young and thin like those models. Why else would mature women buy expensive clothes? All it does is make you poor!

You might accomplish the same thing with a very affordable T-shirt that says it all: "Young at heart, slightly older in other places."

Janice, 47, was excited about the nice watch she received from her family for her 40th birthday, "then was stunned when I saw the brand name was *Fossil*. I thought it was a joke about my age, but my relatives hadn't even made the connection until they saw the look on my face!"

Kathy, 46, worries that she hasn't got a clear picture of what others see when they look at her either. "I *think* I look better now than I did twenty years ago. Am I in denial or what?" Remember the birthday card I received, cautioning me, "At your age it's hard to get new parts"? That warning might have a special meaning to Brenda from Ohio, whose husband ordered a replacement part for their lawn mower. "When I went to the mailbox on my birthday and found a box addressed to me from the Sears Parts Department, my first thought was, *Sears automatically sends spare parts to people when they turn 35!*"

I think women can be divided into two groups: those who are proud to tell you their age—honestly—at the drop of a hat, and those for whom admitting one's age is like confessing to a crime they didn't commit: It's simply *not done*. Elaine, 56, calls it "a whispered age."

I'm among the blurt-it-all-out bunch. 42, 42, 42. So there. Handle it.

My friend Gail is in the "pick-any-number-as-long-as-it's-low" group. When I called to tell her I was including one of her many clever remarks in this book and needed her age (just to be fair—

I had everyone else's), I could feel her blushing over the phone lines. "Do I *have* to tell?" she sighed. Many minutes later, she finally whispered her age to me, and I knew our friendship had taken a quantum leap forward.

Angie Dickinson knew just what to say when a reporter tried to tactfully determine her age by saying, "I'm afraid I forgot how old you are."

"So have I!" Angie shot back.

Another reporter once sent a celebrity a short telegram: "How old Cary Grant?"

The answer was equally brief: "Old Cary Grant fine. How you?"

I figure, as long as people keep saying, "Oh, you look so good," why not just believe them?

The Good News Is . . .

You can always take a lesson from your grandmother and drape all your mirrors as if someone had passed on. Give yourself a little time to mourn the demise of your youth. Cry over photos taken on that one skinny day back in 1971. Go ahead and boo-hoo about the wrinkle-free face of your first two decades, the luxuriant hair of Christmas past, the 20/20 vision of long ago.

There now. Feel better?

Trust me, the day will come when you'll yank the fabric off those mirrors with a flourish and say, "Hello, Gorgeous!" The people who love you most (if they have any sense at all) will agree with you completely.

REASON 22

"Skin Tag" is
not a
playground
game for kids.

"SKIN TAG" IS NOT A PLAYGROUND GAME FOR KIDS.

I had never even heard of the phrase until I eavesdropped on a woman whispering it to her hairstylist: "Skin tag." Is this a sport? A tag team event? A luggage tag made out of (ugh) some animal skin? A name tag that adheres to your skin so it won't ruin your silk blouse? I shot a sideways glance in her direction, hoping she'd have one of these "skin tags" in her hand. She was pointing at her collarbone. Well, what does that mean? What could a "skin tag" have to do with your body? I would soon find out.

One innocent morning, scrubbing my face with mud and sand—well, that's what the stuff feels like—I discovered a tiny flap of skin under my fingertips. It looked flimsy enough to just pinch off like a wilted flower.

OUCH!

Welcome to skin tags. Odd little sacks you can barely hold between your fingers. If you haven't seen one yet, you will. Necks are a happy hunting ground for skin tags. Look for a tiny pocket of flesh the size of a gnat. Juli, 39, from Ohio has found them, too: "Tag moles appear on my body from nowhere!"

Where do these unwelcome flaps of skin come from? Do they happen in your sleep? If you get up an hour earlier, could you catch one before it pops out? Maybe that's why that "Total Woman" swathed herself in Saran Wrap: She was into skin tag prevention.

I've thought about cutting off the half dozen or so little body snatchers that have appeared since I turned 40. Just a quick "snip," then slap on a piece of tissue like a guy who cuts himself while shaving. My skin has clearly indicated that this would be dangerous, even fatal, and definitely messy.

Maybe we should be counting our skin tags. Do you call a doctor when you have, say, fifteen? Will they ever be sexy, like facial moles were in the fifties? Women drew them on with eyeliner pencils, just over the corner of their lip where Marilyn Monroe had hers, remember? (Of course you do, you're over 40.)

Since we can't *draw* a skin tag and get the same effect, perhaps we could cover the most promising parts of our bodies with paper clips every night, hoping to stimulate spontaneous skin tag growth while we sleep. I can see the marketing potential opportunity already: The Skin Tag Club for Women.

Okay, it is a ridiculous idea. Skin tags are not sexy. Skin tags are weird. Rebecca knows maturity means, "age spots and skin tags, just like my grandmother." Skin tags are simply another facet of your post-40 life that qualifies as "bad news." As Margaret from Arizona puts it, "40 is when you start coping with a body that has decided to do what it wants—sag, wrinkle, store fat, and, in general, fall apart."

Or, in this case, flap out.

The Good News Is . . .

Skin tags are not a contagious disease, a fatal illness, or a portent of terrible things to come. Plus, you can't even see them from three feet away. So stand back, stand tall, and cheer up: Almost *every* body plays the skin tag game.

My husband decided to surprise me on my 40th birthday with a full "spa day" at a very posh place. Not wanting to hurt his feelings (and not having a clue as to what I was in for), I dragged myself out of bed at 6:00 A.M. on the one day I would really have loved to sleep late. A full "spa day" might be heaven to some people, but by noon I was wishing I was at home on the couch with my cat lying on my belly, *The Young and the Restless* on the tube, a Diet Coke in one hand, and a bag of Soft Batch cookies by my side. That's what I did on the day *after* my 40th birthday, with the prettiest toenails you ever saw.

Cathy from Kentucky, 40

REASON 23

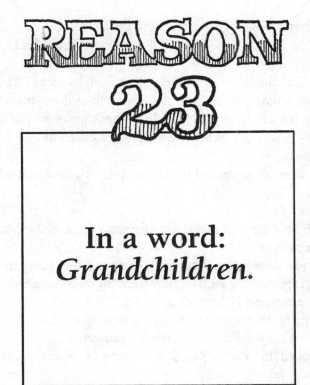

In a word:
Grandchildren.

IN A WORD: *GRANDCHILDREN*.

Children's children are a crown to the aged.

Proverbs 17:6 NIV

Our children's school celebrates Grandparents Day, a day in which Mom and Dad are not even allowed on the school grounds, but *are* required to send in refreshments for the senior attendees. I was out of town the day they called to give us our assignment.

"What are we supposed to take in, Bill?" I asked him when I got home.

"Plates."

"With little chicken salad sandwiches on them, or ham on biscuits, or tuna salad?"

"No, just plates, Liz. When they realized I was going to be in charge of sending the stuff in, they went for something basic they thought a man could handle. So, plates."

Fearing his taste even in something so simple, I asked him tentatively, "What kind of, uh, plates did you get?"

He rolled his eyes. "Plates with pictures of old people on them."

I deserved that. And someday, I'll deserve grandchildren.

Ask any group of women what they like best about midlife, and the response is nigh to unanimous: "Grandbabies!" Since the average age for first-time grandmothers is 46, this could indeed be *your* big decade. Unless you're an older mother with younger children, in which case you *pray every day* that you won't hit grandmother status for a long time.

If my Lillian waits as many years as I did to be fruitful and multiply, I won't be a grandmother until I'm 70. Come and see your old granny Higgs, kiddies. I'll have my hearing aid all tuned up for you.

Ron, 48, says, "If you need proof that you don't have the energy you think you have, let your three grandchildren stay the weekend." Julia teaches preschoolers and admits "it's a challenge to keep my motor going, not to mention getting up from the floor. The kids love to ask me, 'What will you be when you grow up, Ms. Julia?'"

You don't have to give birth to have grandbabies. Becky, 38, works with youngsters of all ages as the children's minister of her church. As a single woman, she's "enjoyed 'mothering' all the kids. As I approach 40, I realize that I'm beginning to look on the babies in a 'grandma' role rather than as a mother. Ouch!"

Our book contributors insist that grandmothering is grand. Carliene loves having "a grandson who lights up every time he sees me. He makes me feel very special and very loved." Barb from Ohio thinks the best part of grandparenting is being able to truly enjoy the grandkids, "and be amused by what they say and do, instead of being embarrassed!"

Case in point: Bill and I went on a dream tenth-anniversary trip to Scotland, leaving our two children, then 7 and 8, in the very able hands of a dear friend. A visit to their paternal grandparents was scheduled for the middle of our bonnie holiday abroad. Around lunchtime in Dumfries (five hours later back home), we found a bright red phone box and started shoving pounds (the coin kind) into the telephone, trying to make a long-distance connection to Kentucky.

No sooner would Bill's parents answer the phone, than the timer would run out and a beeper would sound, indicating it was time to feed the phone again. (Picture a woman my size leaning out of a phone booth shouting, "More pounds! More pounds!")

Our conversation was disjointed at best, but it soon became clear there'd been an "incident" concerning Lillian. "Lilly did not have a good day at school," was the first clue. A garbled phrase followed, then the operator jumped on the line, and more pounds got jammed into the coin slot, just in time to hear my mother-in-law say, "Picked her up at the principal's office after she . . ." and the line went dead again.

Several pounds (and poundings) later, the phone cooperated long enough for us to grasp the whole sordid story.

Maybe it was May, spring fever, end of the year, we don't know what all, but our daughter had the urge to try something that would *really* get someone's attention: She pointed at another child with a finger not generally considered polite to use for pointing.

Oh my.

Please understand, the child had *no earthly idea* what such a gesture meant, but she quickly discovered that pointing like that made the adults at her nice Christian school practically swoon. By the time our in-laws had picked her up in the car-pool line, four or five notes were sticking out of her book bag and Lillian herself was proudly proclaiming, "Guess what I did today?"

The silence across the ocean was deafening. "Mom," I said wearily, "I hope you know she didn't learn such a vulgar gesture from *us!*"

Long pause. Too long. "Well, we didn't think so. Kids just pick up these things." My mother-in-law, a veteran of public school teaching, has been around the block a few times.

I let out a long sigh of relief. "Sorry you've had to deal with this while we're gone, Mom. Is everything else okay?"

"Well, it may be a while before our neighbors speak to us. Lillian was so proud of herself, she couldn't wait to tell them all about it. Complete with a demonstration."

I gulped loudly. "You mean those nice people who used to own the Christian bookstore?" My voice was faint, my face pale.

"The very ones. Actually, they thought it was hysterical."

Oh great. My daughter has torn our parental reputation to shreds and had them rolling in the aisles, all in one day. Our in-laws might agree with Janice from North Dakota who said, "Your grandchildren make you happy twice: once when they come and once when they leave."

But then you'd miss all the hilarious stuff they say. Martha and her recently potty-trained grandson were heading down the highway together:

> I said, "Boy I really have to go to the potty," knowing he would find the subject of interest. A few miles later I said, "I really have to go! I sure hope I don't wet my pants!"
>
> Andrew leaned over toward me and in a confidential tone said, "Don't worry, Grandma, it's okay. I wet my pants yesterday!"

Martha, 54

Your grandchildren make you happy twice: Once when they come and once when they leave.

Of course, having grandchildren isn't always filled with funny, Kodak-perfect moments. Pat from Michigan finds it hard to "watch how young parents raise their kids and wish you could tell them how." Even without grandkids yet, I have to bite my tongue to keep from offering unsolicited advice to young moms at the grocery store.

For Jan from Vermont, whose parents have both died, "there are so many questions I'd love to ask, but can't. I would like to see their smiles of approval and pride as they watch their grandchildren grow." Having buried my own mother nearly twenty years ago, I identify with those longings, too.

The Good News Is . . .

In grandparenting, as in all things, we muddle through with many questions unanswered, many words swallowed whole, grateful for any occasion that brings a child rushing in our direction to throw their arms around our neck.

REASON 24

You won't need
a photo ID to
prove you're
over 21.

YOU WON'T NEED A PHOTO ID TO PROVE YOU'RE OVER 21.

My husband and I don't really worry that much about our age. I have been completely gray since I was 38, and David, 45, has quite a bit of gray in his beard and mustache. We were at Captain D's recently, and when we got our receipt, we saw that the waitress had taken 10 percent from our bill. She'd given us the senior discount! We got so tickled, we could hardly finish our meal! We thought of several things to say to her ("What is the meaning of this, you young whippersnapper!"), but finally decided to just take the discount and enjoy it!

Carol, 44

It doesn't get any easier when you really *do* qualify for those discounts. Jeanne moans, "My Medicare card came in the mail. That was more traumatic than any of the birthdays past! Did they have to send it four months early?" Dick has his AARP card ready, and still "they ask for my driver's license, too. It seems like yesterday that I was carded because I wasn't old enough to get into nightclubs. Now I don't look old enough to get those AARP hotel discounts!"

My least favorite ID cards are the ones with my mug shot on them. Ugh. Methinks I am not alone in this. When I stood in line for my passport photos last spring, I didn't hear one person jump up and say, "Wow! This picture of me is awesome! Quite a camera you've got there. Do you do enlargements?"

Are you kidding? Passport photos are intentionally awful, so the customs people will snap the passport folder shut and hustle you through the line, lest you leave any "ugly" cells behind in their country.

One thing that had better be accurate on such documentation is your age. The government has zero sense of humor about these things. Ann, 54, admits, "I have, on rare occasions, deducted a few years from my age on various nongovernmental forms (that is, those not punished by jail terms). Sometimes it does test the brain cells to recall where I might have taken liberties."

Bev from California has a simple solution, though it won't work indefinitely: "I tell people my age and bra size are the same." That'll keep 'em guessing. Susan, 40, simply says, "I'm 'thirty through' and people think I am saying '33'!" Personally, I announce that I'm the square root of 1,764. Unless they've got a calculator handy, I'm home free.

The Good News Is . . .

I have found a role model for us all, a Texas beauty who said good-bye to 40 some twenty-five years ago and has since had more fun than the law should allow.

Bonnie is a tall, gorgeous, outgoing, life-of-the-party kind of woman, for whom meeting celebrities is just another fun event in her busy day. Her husband was "Big Medicine" in the military, which gave Bonnie some unique opportunities to travel and rub shoulders with the rich and famous:

> *President and Mrs. Carter's plane, Air Force One, was to depart our military base where Jack was commander. As President Carter, a fellow southerner, approached me, I grinned and said, "Hello, sir, I'm from Alabama!" He stopped and said, "Oh, where?" My mind went blank. I couldn't think of one city.*
>
> *(Maybe that's because I grew up on a farm!)*
>
> *While entertaining Air Force Major General Bodycomb in our home, I inadvertently said, "Would you like more coffee, General Goodbody?"*

Baseball hero Jim Palmer was in town promoting his new ladies' Jockey undies. There I was during the sports segment of the local evening news, gazing at him as he autographed my new Jockey briefs!

Finally, I met Fabio and he said to me, "Hello, Luv!" So far the 60s are fabulous (and so is Fabio!).

Does Bonnie make maturity sound fun, or what?

I managed to soak my pastor and the local bookstore owner with underground sprinklers as they were trying to toilet paper the trees. They'd already erected a billboard, chained to trees in front of our house, saying: "Honk to wish Dee a Happy 40th!" We live on a main thoroughfare, so the honking continued all day! Friends arrived at 6:00 A.M., dressed in black mourning clothes and carrying wilted roses, to take me in my flannel nightgown to breakfast. Request time on the local Christian radio station was filled with birthday wishes and songs such as "We've Come This Far by Faith" and "Sweeter as the Years Go By." My full-of-fun Christian bookstore manager took out a newspaper ad for my books at "40 cents off," with comments from local residents like, "I thought she was already 40!"

Dee Brestin,
author of The Friendships of Women

REASON 25

"Saving for a house" has become "saving for retirement."

"SAVING FOR A HOUSE" HAS BECOME "SAVING FOR RETIREMENT."

I always thought a "portfolio" was a leather pouch that held sketches and paintings. So, when my banker inquired about the status of my investment portfolio, I said, "Are you kidding? I can't draw a straight line!"

He quietly closed his file folder and thanked me for stopping by.

My insurance agent, on the other hand, took a deep breath and tried to explain it all to me. After an hour of dizzying statistics and fine print legalese, I sighed and said, "So basically, we give you all the money we have left at the end of each year, and you try not to spend it all before we hit retirement, is that it?"

She smiled and took my check. We now had a portfolio. Imagine that! A couple who thought "no-load" meant a washer that emptied the wet clothes into the dryer by itself, now playing the stock market like a violin.

When quarterly statements arrive, we go straight to the last number: "Oh good, it went up!" or "Oh no, it went down!" Then we throw them away.

I'm amused by the ads that tout, "Make your money work for you." I think our money just got downsized out of a job. Sometimes the only activity on the statement is the service fee.

Best I can tell, you can do about as well by stuffing your money in your couch. Unless your kids are still jumping on it, in which case a coffee can works better. Beware the gold-embossed investment folios with this little verse discreetly printed in the corner: "Cast but a glance at riches, and they are gone."[15] Trust me, this is a portent of things to come.

I'm just grateful that Bill and I could even come to a point of agreement about how to invest our limited resources. To say that the two of us have similar philosophies about money would be like suggesting that Dolly and Twiggy have almost the same measurements.

Bill is tight and I'm not. He likes to count money, I like to spend money. He likes to save money, I like to give it away. Women worry, *Will my husband be faithful?* Men worry, *Can I trust her with the money?* I try my best to be trustworthy. Bill tries his best never to give me the checkbook.

An audience member once shared that her mother always kept a red ink pen in the glove compartment. When her mom returned home from a shopping spree and was safely parked in the driveway, she'd pull out all the tags and mark them down herself!

Is this what the Scripture means about the older women teaching the younger women?!

Family vacations tax our financial differences to the limit, since I'm a Ritz Carlton girl and Bill's a Motel 6 guy. A 1993 trip to Alaska was the last of our budget vacations, thanks to one seriously seedy-looking motel.

"They said they were doing a little remodeling," Bill offered, trying to sound hopeful. Or maybe apologetic. We all climbed out of the car, while he headed for the sign marked "Office" swinging just above the door sporting "Coors Alaska" in neon. I tried to shield the children so they wouldn't see their father walking into a bar to get our room key.

Forgive us, Lord. We didn't know.

The Denali View Motel defies description, but let me try. Imagine a small church camp built in the 1940s and long since abandoned, featuring paneled walls that speak of good stewardship with limited funds. The interior design might best be summed up as "orange."

I, on the other hand, saw red.

You'll be happy to know that for our tenth-anniversary trip to Scotland, my sweet Bill booked only the finest B&B's, from Islesteps to Inverness. Money was no object. I was so proud of him.

Harriet from Louisiana spent her 40th birthday on a romantic cruise "until the ship we were on was hit broadside by a Greek freighter. Does this mean that life after 40 is like a sinking ship going down for the third time?"

Kay is a pediatrician who has spent a lifetime working sixteen-hour days, nights, and weekends. "The fear of retirement in terms of having enough money saved to last to the end has been the biggest challenge the last ten years, until I finally learned to trust an unknown future to a known God!"

Her retirement concerns are heightened by the fact that she is "one of those single women who never married. I miss having children of my own, but as a pediatrician, I have had many kids!"

Kay would enjoy a book by author and buddy Harold Ivan Smith called *Fortysomething and Still Single* (Victor Books, 1991). He points out that for the childless woman who is turning 40, "she may feel caught between a clock and a hard place." Family is an investment, too, of time, money, and every other resource available. Like financial investments, there are no guarantees on this one either.

Every woman imagines "what if." *What if I'm suddenly widowed or divorced? How would I handle it? Would I marry again?* Judith, 53, paints a gloomy picture of dating as a midlife single woman, revealing that "you have to date everyone's leftovers. Most men date younger women. To be the younger woman, I'd have to date 70 year olds. One man my own age said I was the oldest woman he'd ever dated!"

Maybe that's why Adrienne, 34, is cutting down her shopping list for a husband rather drastically. Now just three items remain. She insists that "under no circumstances will I date a man who has smaller feet than me, who owns anything that sheds its skin, or who drives a car that wears a bra!"

The Good News Is . . .

If you're facing your 40s without a husband by your side, you can invest in Safe-T Man, available from a catalog company near you!

Why drive around alone at night, when you can have a polyester-filled cotton torso sitting next to you? So reassuring. So convincing. So macho, with his puffed-out chest that doubles as a pincushion.

There are a few glitches here. He has "realistically sandy hair," so you'll have to let go of the "tall, dark, and handsome" fantasy. Oh, he appears to be tall—six feet—but only weighs four pounds. Don't try to sit in his lap.

Legs are extra—$19.50 to be exact—which you won't need in the car, but might be useful if you two plan to go dancing. Clothing is not included, so throw modesty out the window when you take him shopping and have to go into the dressing room with him.

And sorry, no two-day delivery. Like most men, it'll take years for him to show up at your doorstep. But hey, at $99.95 (or four interest-free payments of $25.00), he's the bargain bachelor of the year, with zero appetite, frugal spending habits, and no interest whatsoever in your retirement fund!

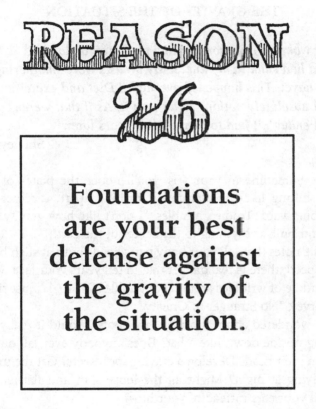

REASON
26

Foundations
are your best
defense against
the gravity of
the situation.

FOUNDATIONS ARE YOUR BEST DEFENSE AGAINST THE GRAVITY OF THE SITUATION.

I woke up one morning and my entire abdominal area had sunk to my knees. My breasts were smothering my navel. This happened overnight! Diet and exercise had absolutely nothing to do with it. As if that weren't bad enough, I had to turn 50 five years later.

Shirley, 51

Sometime in your 40s, you'll notice the plates of your body shifting like the continents, drifting apart, together, and ever southward. Trudie grumbles, "I don't like how gravity takes over and pulls everything to the center of the earth."

Ninie notes that "all your body parts head south at such breakneck speed, there is real danger that in ten years your face will lie in a puddle of wrinkles around your ankles." Patt, 47, just signed her survey, "No Stranger to Gravity."

I've wondered about those gravity boots. Would it really help to hang upside down like a bat? Does anybody ever fall out and land on their head? Develop a craving for insects? Get the urge to start flying at night? Might all the loose skin and flab end up around your ears instead of your hips?

Patty from Oklahoma "heard a joke a long time ago, that after 40 you get the 'Chest of Drawers' disease: Your chest falls into your drawers! Well, guess what . . . ?" Linda, 48, agrees that the tricky thing "is trying to keep my breasts from touching the top of my thighs! And trying to find an undergarment that will do the job, especially when the salesgirl is a Barbie look-alike."

Please note: Barbie's birthday is March 1, 1959. The old girl is almost 40 herself and still maintains her youthful (surreal) figure.

Martha from Indiana has done some research, and contends that, "Our bodies do have a tendency to literally let us down! I have conducted a visual survey of behinds. Men's posteriors, as they age, are re-absorbed and pooch out at the tummy, while women's behinds have the unfortunate tendency to ripple down their leg!"

As the saying goes, "A waist is a terrible thing to mind." Good thing, because after 40, you'd better not mind losing your waist. Ellen, 43, has spent many hours "searching for just the right belt for every outfit, so I can pretend I still have a waist." Susan declares, "My waistline disappeared! One day I could fit in all my skirts and the next I lost half of my wardrobe!"

Your favorite hymn is "How Firm a Foundation."

My own foundations are so industrial strength I have to order them from catalogs. After ordering one underwire brassiere after another, only to have the wires sticking out and poking me in the ribs in no time, I finally sent a dozen of them back to the company with a note that just said, "I think you should know that your bras poke me."

Lo and behold, the next catalog comes out and what do they have advertised now? A "No-Poke" bra! I kid you not, that was the *name* of the thing! The ad copy even said, "Here's a bra that won't poke you like those other ones do." I couldn't believe it! They also sent me a check for a *full refund* on the dozen bras. Honey, you know that *never* happens. A firmer foundation and no poking. I am one happy "DD" camper.

Foundational garments won't be the least bit helpful to Deana, 43, who is fretting over her sagging *chins*. "I haven't taken a picture in years without reminding all my 40-something friends to 'chin up!'"

Alvarie, 46, says, "I expected most things on my body would sag with time but never would've guessed my *earlobes* would sag." Her advice? "Pierce your daughter's ears higher so she can still wear pierced earrings at 40!"

The Good News Is . . .

So what if you can't run around in the nude without knocking things over with runaway flab. Who cares? Did you really want to be seen naked anyway? Of course not. Dressed, you can still look smashing. Never mind diamonds: Foundations are a girl's best friend.

Faye, 41, has an outlook that can't be beat:

All those years of wishing and hoping for a well-rounded, shapely body have come to pass. Problem is, the rounding part happened in the wrong places, and gravity is taking its toll on what shape is left. On the brighter side, I know my resurrected body will be magnificent. Amen!

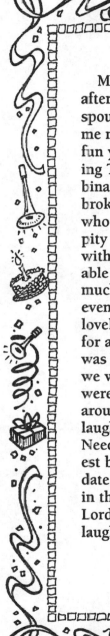

My birthday fell just one week after foot surgery, and just after my spouse of sixteen years had given me notice and left. Are we having fun yet? My sister was administering TLC and aspirin—a great combination for a throbbing foot and a broken heart. Another dear friend who is a Mary Kay consultant took pity on me and came over to play with my face! We all had an enjoyable afternoon and my face showed much improvement. Later that evening a wonderful friend and my lovely sister loaded me into the car for a trip to the state fair where I was then placed in a golf cart and we went "free wheelin'." There we were, the three of us, tooling around the fairgrounds, munching, laughing, and popping "wheelies." Needless to say this was the craziest birthday I have celebrated to date! It's so nice to know that even in the midst of difficult trials the Lord chooses to bless us with laughter and joy!

Julye from Kentucky, 40

REASON 27

You can afford
a good
therapist.

YOU CAN AFFORD A GOOD THERAPIST.

You will *not* suddenly go off the deep end emotionally when you turn 40. It'll just seem that way. Bonnie, 43, is a teacher who admits, "I can be reading a story to my students and just start crying for no reason. My students will ask what is wrong and I'll say, 'I don't know!' We have a lot of good laughs about my crying."

Yes, life after 40 is all about leaking. Sometimes I feel like an expectant mother watching a Kodak commercial, tears pouring down my cheeks without a second's warning. Both crying jags have the same source: hormones. Peggy, 46, finds it tough staying on track while riding a "midlife, premenopausal, emotional roller coaster on its way to the big 5-0!" There's up ("Hooray, an empty nest!"), there's down ("Oh no, college tuition!"), and there's upside down ("Your mother is moving in *when*?").

Shirley from California remembers the mercurial nature of those years: "In her 40s, a woman can feel very torn. Until age 47, I raised my six children all alone, working several teaching jobs to support them. At the same time my parents demanded so much from me. I had no time for 'me,' that's for sure."

For some women, turning 40 means *more* time for yourself, and for others *less* time to take care of your own needs. More time may make us feel guilty—"Is it really okay to expect the kids to pack their own lunches?"—and less time may produce resentment—"How come my mother can't just do meals-on-wheels like everybody else?"

Read my lips: Taking a bit of time to meet your physical, emotional, social, intellectual, and spiritual needs is more than just a good idea, it's an absolute must. One hour each week of the year I turned 40, I carved out some "time for me" and spent it with a terrific therapist. Nothing earth-shattering, just clean up work, sorting out old hurts and shaking off dysfunctional cling-ons. It was the best 40th birthday gift I could have given myself. Sure wish I could have made that investment at age 20 or 30, but it took forty years to realize it's okay to ask for help.

It also took forty years to save up the money to pay for it.

One useful lesson that I learned was how to have an adult temper tantrum in the privacy of your own home. Has your boss made your life miserable again? Did your teenager just tell you how idiotic you are? Is your outfit for Saturday night suddenly two sizes too small?

Here's the therapeutic approach: Dig out a tennis racket or baseball bat from the garage and march to your bedroom. (Try not to bop any family members on the bean while charging by, no matter how tempting.)

Close the door, take a deep breath, position yourself at the end of the bed, and start whacking that mattress for all you're worth. *Thwomp! Blam! Thwomp! Blam!* When you get a good rhythm going, add sound effects. No bad words, please, just some giant sumo-wrestler-type grunts and growls: "Arrrggh! Raaahhrr! Heeeuhhh!"

Do you look and sound ridiculous? Of course. But not as ridiculous as you'd look venting your spleen at your boss, your child, or that shrunken dinner dress. By having a "controlled" tantrum—on your terms, in your room, with only God as your witness—you can work out all your anger and frustration in advance, then face the trigger situation calmly and angst-free.

Note: Plan to buy a new mattress every few years. It's cheaper than another year in therapy.

Since my sweet daughter, Lillian, is so much like me in temperament, I decided to teach her the fine art of mattress thwacking after we had the following conversation when she was 7:

> Liz: "*Young lady, you are too old to be throwing a temper tantrum!*"
> Lillian: "*But, Mom, it's my only talent: Acting!*"

Now when Lillian is feeling the urge to cut loose, she announces, "I'm going to my room to slug my pillow!" She stomps up the steps, appearing a few minutes later, clear-eyed and joyful again. This therapeutic thwacking works.

My mother had her own time-tested solution to the stress of raising six children: She would create bizarre things in the basement. The olive shadow box that ended up in the upstairs bathroom, for starters. It was about three feet tall and two feet wide, made out of cardboard painted with green antiquing—awful stuff, but very sixties. Inside she suspended wax shapes formed from candles that dripped into fascinating blobs. Think "framed lava lamp." When my friends asked, "What is *that*?" I was always proud to tell them my mother made such *objets d'art* in her very own, one-person art therapy class.

"Isn't it funky?" I'd add, beaming. "She's really cool, for a mom." Since I didn't arrive in my mother's life until after she was 40, her roller-coaster ride into menopause seemed perfectly normal to me, and her art was a natural way to work out life's mood-altering kinks.

The Good News Is . . .

Time is its own form of therapy. It heals and renews us. It teaches us things about ourselves. A Minnesota woman puts it all in perspective:

The best thing about turning 40 is that I started to live in the present! I realized all the "what if" details didn't matter. This is my life. Right here, right now. It's wonderfully liberating and the world would be a better place if this happened to us in our 20s! I waited a long time to feel this good. Every year gets better for me.

Patt, 47

REASON 28

Your mother
visits you every
day . . . in your
mirror.

YOUR MOTHER VISITS YOU EVERY DAY . . .
IN YOUR MIRROR.

There's one woman who knows your exact age, to the hour, better than you do: Your mother. After all, she was there. Maybe even conscious.

When I turned 40, I cried all day and didn't want anyone wishing me a Happy Birthday. My mom stopped by and I burst out in tears. When she asked me what was wrong, I told her, "It's this 40th birthday." She said, "You're not 40, you're only 39! I should know, I'm your mother." She was right. My real 40th didn't bother me at all!

Shirley, 56

Is this what they mean by "short-term memory loss"?

I was 5 when my mother turned 48, so remembering her age was easy: It was the same as the number on my box of Crayolas. She stayed 48 for several years, then suddenly leaped to 64 when I wanted the box with a crayon sharpener on the back.

This Kentucky woman may be following in her mother's footsteps.

At five minutes till midnight, I calmly announced that I was 49 years old, then went to bed before anyone could tell me I was 50. Later that day I couldn't find my glasses. I remembered exactly where I put them before showering, but they just weren't there. I'd been 50 for eight hours and already I'd lost my short-term memory! I wore my prescription sunglasses for four hours before

my mother discovered she had mistaken my glasses for
hers and put them in her purse.

Priscilla, 50

Solomon must have been over 40 when he wrote, "Listen to
your father, who gave you life, and do not despise your mother
when she is old."[16] He clearly understood the volatile adult-to-
adult relationships that develop between women and their parents: Sometimes you find a gold mine, sometimes a land mine.

It really gets scary when you realize you're turning *into* your
parents. Janet from California struggles with "seeing my mother's
chin on my face or wondering who that old woman is looking
back at me." Pamela from Kentucky agrees that "the hardest part
is finding my mother in so many mirrors, especially the three-
way mirrors in department stores. I wonder why she didn't tell
me she was going shopping, too, and when did she buy a suit like
mine and . . . oh!"

I don't see my mom when I look in the mirror, I see my father.
(And boy, does he look funny in a dress!) I have his chin(s), his
smile, his nose, the whole deal. But when I look at my sister
Sarah, there's our mother, one more time.

I'm grateful to see Mom's image reflected in one of the six of
us, since she's been gone from this earth for almost twenty years,
God rest her soul. In the early weeks of 1978, the chronic cough
that had haunted her for years finally had a name: emphysema.
A hospital became her home. Eager to bring some cheer her way,
one day in February I sneaked in a Hershey's chocolate bar, her
favorite.

"Will the doctors mind?" I asked with concern.

"They'll never see it!" she assured me, opening the wrapper
with all the enthusiasm of a child.

The last day I saw her alive was Mother's Day. Daddy had
brought her home from the hospital, determined to let her enjoy
her last months, or days, surrounded by the things and the people that she loved. Wanting to be helpful, I ran the vacuum

around and cooked a dreadful dinner of burned hamburger steak and hard green peas. She loved it. She even ate it.

Four days later, Daddy and my brother Tom appeared at the door of my apartment. The minute I saw them, dressed in blue suits on a Thursday afternoon, I knew my mother was gone.

Not all of us get another chance at having a mom. My dear dad mourned for her as long as he could stand being alone, then began courting a woman that he and Mom had both known. A few months later, down the aisle they went. To say that Mary is a blessing to our family is an understatement. Since day one she's made Daddy go for long, healthy walks, and she stuffs him with prunes to keep him regular. A fine stepmother indeed, our Mary.

But she lived in Pennsylvania, and here I was in Kentucky, a single woman those fourteen years ago, wishing I had a real flesh-and-blood mom. Enter Doris.

The first time I laid eyes on Doris she was sitting on a chintz-covered couch, ukulele in hand, leading a dozen women in song. To be honest, I thought she was weird.

No doubt about it, God has a sense of humor: Within a few weeks, Doris became my "foster mother," a role that suits her well, since her last name is "Foster"!

Doris did those things a real mother might do: She fed me dinner often and served my favorite chocolate nut sheet cake for dessert. She hung a stocking with my name on it from the mantel at Christmas, and included me in their many Foster gatherings. Thanks to Doris, I felt loved, accepted, and encouraged. In a word, I felt like *family*.

Now that I'm sufficiently grown up to function without a mother's constant care, Doris has gradually moved into the role of friend. My stocking hasn't been hung by her chimney with care for a decade, and my calls "home" have grown fewer and farther apart.

But in fact I'm acting more like my foster mom everyday. I've found myself playing hymns on my dulcimer, my own hair is turning silver, and I'm always on the lookout for someone who needs a little "maternal encouragement." A woman just can't have too many mothers.

The Good News Is . . .

When you look in the mirror, you may see your mother. When she looks at you, what does she see? Betty writes:

> *This is the year my daughter turns 40, which has prompted some pleasant reminiscing for us When I turned 40, I was busy being mother to a 4 year old and to the smartest teenager in the world. She was convinced she had the earliest curfew of the entire school, the worst clothes, the smallest allowance, the fewest driving privileges, the strictest mother, and in general, the worst set of parents a girl could get stuck with. Luckily, she matured and I mellowed. Now I have the loveliest, smartest, most sensitive, caring daughter who has given me two beautiful grandbabies and a very nice son-in-law. I'm proud to call her friend, but even more proud to call her daughter.*

The greatest gift we can give our moms, whether they became our mothers via birth, adoption, step, or foster, is to mirror not only their faces, but also their lives, adding a few wrinkles of our own to pass on to our daughters who even now peer at themselves in the mirror saying, "Oh no! Is that you, Mom?"

I thought our plans were to go shopping and then come home for a quiet birthday dinner—alone. Instead, as soon as we left, twenty of my family and friends began arriving with all the makings of a party. As they started putting up balloons and arranging the food they heard noises in the kitchen— my mother-in-law had proceeded to take my stove apart and clean it! Honest, my stove wasn't that bad. (She has two quirks: obsessive tidiness and the need to purchase items on sale and then use her key to our house to drop them off.) When we arrived after dark to a dimly lit house, I walked into the kitchen and noticed a paper bag on the table. The first thing out of my mouth (in a somewhat sarcastic tone) was, "Well, your mother's been here." With that, the lights came on, a shout of "Surprise!" rang out, and guess who was the first one down the hall? My mother-in-law, of course!

Gale from Kentucky, 39

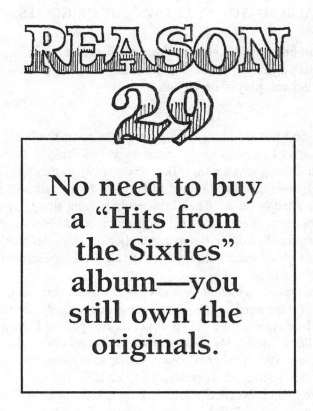

REASON 29

No need to buy a "Hits from the Sixties" album—you still own the originals.

NO NEED TO BUY A "HITS FROM THE SIXTIES" ALBUM—YOU STILL OWN THE ORIGINALS.

You know you're getting older when you're in the dentist's office and hear your favorite rock song from high school, played on violins.

Bea, 40

So I was standing at the teller's window at the bank, feeling smug as I listened to the piped-in Muzak, rolling from one Elton John song into another. *They don't even know they just played two of his tunes in a row!* I thought to myself. In my radio DJ days, that was a major no-no. Then I started humming along, trying to remember how the lyrics went, and drew a blank. Hm-m. Pretty soon I realized I couldn't even remember the *titles*, let alone the words. Maybe it wasn't Elton John after all. Paul McCartney? Rod Stewart? Oh dear.

There was a time when we knew every word, every wail, every wa-wa in every song our teen idols sang. Suzanne, 47, confesses, "In my hometown, it all boiled down to: Are you an Elvis girl or a Pat Boone girl? My God-fearing, women's-club-belonging, apple-pie-baking mother set out to make sure I was not a fan of anyone whose middle name was 'The Pelvis.'"

Jackie, 49, is worried about her own kids because "they're studying about the Beatles in Music *History* class, and I was there when it happened!" Betty admits that she, too, is "old enough to know that an 8-track is not a utility vehicle."

Gale had a run-in with two "Generation X-ers" that put it all in perspective for her:

My company sent me to Pittsburgh for a training session. One evening after dinner, we noticed a large gathering of people at the riverfront down below. As we got

closer, we heard music playing and I commented how
much it sounded like Bob Dylan. When we got back to
our car, we realized we had left the lights on and the
battery was dead. Fortunately, a young couple (probably 19–20 years old) stopped to help us.

As the guys began working under the hood, the
young woman asked me, "Were you at the concert,
too?"

"No," I replied, "but we heard the music. Who was
singing?"

With that, her eyes lit up: "BOB DYLAN!" Then,
with a gasp of excitement she added, "Oh my gosh! You
were from his era, weren't you? Did you go to
Woodstock?!"

Granted, I'm twenty years older than her, but
Woodstock? I was in the seventh grade during
Woodstock!

My mother wouldn't even let me go see the movie *Woodstock* because it was rated "M" for mature audiences. Remember that? We bought the album, we learned the Fish Cheer, but most of us didn't get much closer to Yasgur's Farm than the six o'clock news. My mom was happier when I was listening to pop, folk, or soul. The Mamas and Papas, Joan Baez, Aretha Franklin, that kind of music. We all had our favorites, but not many of us could say we had this happen on our 40th birthday.

> *Ever since I was 10, my singing idol has been Mark Lindsey of Paul Revere and the Raiders. I first saw him on the show,* Where the Action Is. *When my husband asked me what I wanted for my 40th birthday, I said to see Mark in concert. It happened! Not only did I see four of his shows, he came to my party and sang "Happy Birthday" to me—a childhood dream come true!*
>
> Cyndy, 40

Gee whiz, I couldn't even get Bill and the kids to sing to me, let alone Tom Jones, Mickey Dolenz, or Gary Puckett, three of my teenage heartthrobs. Truth be told, I haven't been to a rock concert in ages. The last one (and I mean the *last* one) was a Rolling Stones concert in 1981. All I remember was Mick looked very skinny and too old for spandex (we had one thing in common) and the music was so loud my ears rang for a week.

When it comes to rock concerts, Carolyn, 49, pretty well sums it up: "The *best* thing about being over 40 is knowing it's okay if you haven't attended a Hootie and the Blowfish concert. The *worst* thing? Not being *invited* to attend a Hootie and the Blowfish concert!"

Music, television, board games, and toys all defined our lives growing up. For kids today, Nintendo and interactive CD-ROMs might be closer to the mark. Just for fun, I thumbed through several collections of hit songs, hot shows, fickle fads, and fond memories, and came up with a quick reference guide to what was fun when we were young. Get ready for a blast from the past, as we review some childhood memories, year by golden year.

In 1950, we sat in our knotty-pine paneled living rooms with Groucho Marx and *You Bet Your Life*, and tried our Silly Putty on the Sunday comics.

In 1951, we unpacked our first color TV just in time for *Red Skelton* and *I Love Lucy*. (I love Lucy, too, though I look more like Ethel Mertz.)

In 1952, we wore paper glasses at 3-D movies, and sighed over Ricky while watching *The Adventures of Ozzie and Harriet*.

In 1953, we kept track of what was on all *three* channels with the new *TV Guide*, and borrowed vegetables from Mom to play with Mr. Potato Head.

In 1954, we begged for a Davy Crockett lunch box, and ate our first of many McDonald's hamburgers.

In 1955, we made two new friends—*Captain Kangaroo* and *The Mickey Mouse Club*, while we discovered the fun of Wiffle Balls.

In 1956, we danced with Dick Clark and *American Bandstand*, screamed at *The Invasion of the Body Snatchers*, and crooned with "Love Me Tender."

In 1957, we asked *The $64,000 Question*, felt right at home with *Leave It to Beaver*, and tossed our first Frisbee.

In 1958, we hopped around singing "Peggy Sue" (or, for those of us with more taste, "The Purple People Eater"), and swirled our hips in Hula Hoops.

In 1959, we shivered at the theme to *The Twilight Zone* (do-do-do-do, do-do-do-do), dressed our Barbie dolls in evening gowns, and tried on a bikini.

In 1960, we did the Twist to those new 45 RPM records, doodled on our first Etch-a-Sketch, and laughed with *The Andy Griffith Show* and *The Flintstones*.

In 1961, we had a crush on *both* Dr. Kildaire and Ben Casey, and tripped over the ottoman every week with Rob Petrie on *The Dick Van Dyke Show*.

In 1962, we watched John Glenn orbit the earth, danced the Mashed Potato, and agreed with Charles Schulz that "Happiness Is a Warm Puppy."

In 1963, we got a little spacey with *My Favorite Martian* and *The Outer Limits*, then played with Troll Dolls that looked like aliens.

In 1964, we went to the World's Fair in New York with our parents, did the Funky Chicken, and bought a GI Joe doll for our brothers for Christmas.

In 1965, we really did *Get Smart* if we owned any of the new must-have items: a lava lamp, a skateboard, a Super ball, or granny glasses.

In 1966, we saw *Star Trek* and *Batman*—the first time, not reruns—and giggled when we tried on go-go boots and paper dresses.

In 1967, we were bowled over by the first Super Bowl, tried to understand *The Graduate*, and got no "R-E-S-P-E-C-T" if we didn't look like Twiggy.

In 1968, we cried at *Romeo and Juliet*, howled at *Rowan and Martin's Laugh-In*, and tried on Nehru jackets and beanbag chairs. Neither one fit.

In 1969, we loved two dynamic duos—*Butch Cassidy and the Sundance Kid* and *The Smothers Brothers*—and watched the moon landing from our water beds.

The Good News Is . . .

Those trends we loved, those songs we sang,
Have all returned to haunt us, gang;
Our TV shows that brought delight,
Are hits again on "Nick-at-Nite."

With bells on pants and platformed toes,
It's déjà vu for all our clothes;
Our songs are all the stations play,
The retro mood is here to stay!

— Liz Curtis Higgs

REASON
30

You remember
the words to
"Chapel of
Love" but not
where you
parked the car.

YOU REMEMBER THE WORDS TO "CHAPEL OF LOVE" BUT NOT WHERE YOU PARKED THE CAR.

Japanese scientists project that by the year 2015, researchers will have discovered a cure for memory loss. I turn 61 that year. I hope I'll remember where I put my medicine.

Memory is one of the first things to go after you pass the big 4-0.

I live in a small town in Ohio where there is only one Main Street. One sunny afternoon I drove downtown, parked my battered Dodge, and went inside my favorite bookstore. After buying several books, I went back outside and could not remember where I had parked my car. I scanned all the cars on Main Street and began to panic. How could any sane person lose their car in this small a town?

I gathered whatever wits I had left and began searching the side streets, to no avail. Now I was really feeling foolish. What should I do? Return to the bookstore and admit, "I've lost my car"?

Or worse yet, call my husband and tell him? NEVER! I decided I would keep my wounded pride and search one more time. And there it was, not on the street at all, but parked in a distant corner of the bank parking lot. I slipped behind the wheel and didn't tell a soul.

Marijane, 54

Ah, but you told all of us, Marijane, and that may be your undoing! I've lost my keys, my car, my purse, my directions, and my glasses, and that was only Tuesday. If memories *are* "like the corners of my mind," I could easily get lost in the middle of the block. This California woman understands:

> *When I turned 40 my friends surprised me with a luncheon party. There'd been a lot of discussion about memory loss at 40. Since I'm very organized, disciplined, and never forget anything, I was beside myself when I couldn't find the keys to my car to join my friends for the luncheon. I searched and searched, then became so upset I decided to stay home. Well, it seems they'd hidden my keys to tease me and also to delay my arrival so they could all be there to surprise me. Only I was so upset over my forgetfulness, I didn't show up! (Finally, they called and I went.)*
>
> **Glenda, 55**

When asked to share their 40th birthday memories, many women couldn't boot up a single byte on their memory screens. Sue, 47, wrote: "My over-40 memory, what's left of it, prohibits me from completing this section." Other women not only can't remember their 40th *now*, they didn't even remember it *then:* "I was so busy working and going back to school I completely forgot it. Two days later I realized the cards piling up on the table were my birthday cards!" wrote Cindy, 41.

Driving to a local radio station for an early morning interview, I went right past the highway exit and drove to the airport. (Talk about being on autopilot!) When I got to the terminal and started digging in my purse for a plane ticket, beads of sweat were pouring down my face before it dawned on me that I'd driven to the wrong place!

Jumping back on the expressway, fighting morning traffic, I listened to the agitated announcer saying, "Well, we *think* Liz Curtis Higgs will be joining us this morning, but still no sign of her. Hope she didn't have an accident on the highway." Oh, I'd had an accident, all right. A front-end collision of the memory bank.

Catherine, 43, admits, "The other day, I was commenting to my son about something the neighbor had added to the landscape. He informed me that we watched him plant it six months ago." And Gayle, 44, says, "My sense of humor improves as my memory collapses, so every day is a new day!"

The apostle Peter wrote, "I think it is right to refresh your memory . . ."[17] Oh please, by all means, freshen it right up. Bill and I help each other in this regard. A lesson learned can sometimes be a lesson forgotten. For example, when we first married, I assured Bill that making coffee was not difficult, that he in fact could learn this valuable skill in four easy steps:

> *Step One: Put the filter in the basket and add coffee.*
> *Step Two: Pour the water in the machine.*
> *Step Three: Push brew.*
> *Step Four: Put the coffeepot under the basket.*

One sleepy, short-term memory lapse morning, guess which step he skipped?

> *If you skip Step One, you have plain hot water.*
> *If you skip Step Two, you have a fried coffeepot.*
> *If you skip Step Three, you have a slight delay before that first cup.*
> *If you skip Step Four, you'll be greeted by the Mocha Java River, flowing across the countertop, down the cabinets, and all over the kitchen floor.*

Sure enough, we were baptized in the river that morning. It won't refresh your taste buds, but it will definitely refresh your memory.

The Good News Is . . .

Some things are *worth* forgetting: Detention hall. Childbirth. That D– in Algebra. Your first boyfriend. How much you've paid in taxes since 1970. Selective memory loss is a handy device.

Things worth remembering just require advance planning: If keys are a problem, make some duplicates (don't forget to tag them, or you'll have to remember what key opens what, too!), and hide a spare set in your purse. Keep putting your purse down and losing it? No problem. Wear one of those new, teeny tiny purses on a long, skinny strap around your neck. Now it's not a purse, it's a necklace. Have trouble remembering phone numbers and such? They make palm-size computers (that fit in those teeny tiny purses) to carry such information with you everywhere you go.

As long as you never change purses, you're all set!

This is how we helped our sister turn 40: She was across the state at a convention and made a big deal about not telling anyone where she would be. My two brothers, sister-in-law, brother-in-law, and I drove all afternoon, changed into clown outfits, brought in rap dance music, and entertained the people at my sister's convention during their prime rib dinner. The troops were sure we were the hired performers! You can only imagine how startled they were when, after we sang "Happy Birthday," we pulled off the clown masks and revealed our secret. It was great! It made the magician, who *was* the hired entertainment, work real hard to earn his wage!

Trudye from South Dakota, 41

REASON 31

Your new name
is "Ma'am."

31

YOUR NEW NAME IS "MA'AM."

From the time we're born, we females are addressed according to our age at any given moment:

At 5, it's "Princess."
At 10, it's "Missy."
At 15, it's "Young Lady."
At 20, it's "Miss."
At 25, it's "Young Woman."
At 30, it's "Ms."
At 35, it's "Mrs." (whether accurate or not).
And at 40, it's "Ma'am." Ouch.

"Ma'am" is short for Madam. Is this supposed to be a compliment? It beats "old lady," "old bag," or "old gray mare," but not by much.

Oh for the days when we were just called by our names, names like Donna, Sue, Kathy, Debbie, Karen—those were the biggies in the Class of '72. Linda was another favorite:

At Christmastime, I invited my three teenage nieces to my house for our annual cookie baking afternoon. The girls were discussing school, and one of them mentioned that she shares a locker with a girl named Linda. Immediately, all three girls started laughing. I asked what was so funny, and the youngest said "Linda?! That's such an old name!" (These girls are Katie, Heather, and Courtney, which sort of sums it all up.) I guess today's Linda is yesterday's Maude!

Patt, 47

Elizabeth was *not* a hip name to have growing up, but is "way cool" now among the nursery set. It was my mother's name, too. The first time I ever used my mother's credit card, I was 19 and feeling very grown up until the clerk addressed me as "Mrs." I almost fainted. "No! No! That's my mother," I protested. Surely I wasn't old enough to be married?!? Never mind that I'd just sung at my best friend's wedding, I was *not* ready to move from Miss to Mrs.!

That first "Ma'am" happened a decade later, after I moved to Louisville. When a gas station attendant said, "Check yer oil, Ma'am?" I was devastated until I later observed that all good southern gentlemen call a woman, "Ma'am," even a younger woman. Of course, now that I'm over 40, I hear "Ma'am" when I travel in the Northeast, the Southwest, the Midwest, Alaska, etc. Mickey remembers the day she realized "I was being addressed as 'Ma'am' at the grocery store—'Will that be paper or plastic,

Ma'am?' At the time, I didn't take it as a sign of respect, but rather, a sign that I was getting older. (I wasn't convinced that I liked it either!)"

A friend made a wickedly funny suggestion: Next time you're on the phone with an obviously younger woman, call her "Ma'am" and see if she doesn't start sputtering. Ooh, now that's cruel! Then there's this Kentucky woman's observation:

> *After 40, 20 year olds call you "Ma'am," 60 year olds call you "Young Lady," and gold-chained party lizards stop calling you altogether.*

Ninie, 48

The Good News Is . . .

As Janet sees it, there are two pluses here: "Today I get a polite 'Ma'am' instead of a whistle and people offer you their seat!"

REASON 32

Friends who "remember you when" . . . don't.

FRIENDS WHO "REMEMBER YOU WHEN" . . . DON'T.

Friend (noun): Someone who cries when you cry, laughs when you laugh, tells you when you have lipstick on your teeth or a run in your panty hose, and never tells a soul your age or dress size.

My friends over the years have stuck with me through thick and thin (thick, mostly). I love when they have a little fun at my expense. It means they love me and know our friendship is secure enough to handle it. As Janet sees it, "At age 6, presents are important; at 60, it's who brings them."

Some of our friendships go way back. It's a hoot watching Lillian learn the art of making friends. At 7, her loyalty to her classmates changes daily. "Sarah is my best friend!" she'll say on Monday, so on Wednesday I suggest we have Sarah over after school. "No way, Mom! She won't talk to me anymore. Can we invite Gracie instead?"

How well we remember. Like Diane, 43, we'd probably agree that one of the advantages of being over 40 is "knowing that you don't have to go through grade school, high school, and the 'best friend' dilemma again." Lynn's daughter was amazed her mother even had any friends, saying in astonishment, "I thought everyone you went to school with was dead by now, Mom!"

Most of us are still alive and kicking, and in many ways, our friends are more important to us now than ever. "Friendships with other women are much more solid," says Sue, 47. "Women are less competitive toward each other, and ready to share all of life's ups and downs. After 40, you really bond with other women."

Leigh, 42, had an especially bonding experience when "my friends woke me at 12:05 A.M. on my 40th birthday carrying dead flowers, black candles, and singing funeral hymns. They stayed until 4:00 A.M., then put toilet paper on every tree and bush in my yard."

In high school our friends applied peer pressure. In our 40s they apply no pressure. You can disagree with a friend now and not worry about losing their vote for senior class secretary. You can cry on a friend's shoulder and know they won't think you're weird (just menopausal). Solomon wisely observed, "If one falls down, his friend can help him up. / But pity the man who falls and has no one to help him up!"[18]

Susie, 42, got a real pick-me-up when she arrived at work on her birthday to discover "my 'friends' had my office appropriately decorated in black, including the large office dictionary opened on my desk with the word *old* highlighted." Theresa, 47, "received a handmade walking stick, a jar of vanishing cream, a package of hearing aid batteries, and several other things that (due to my advanced age!) I have forgotten." You know what they say: With friends like that . . . Martha from Indiana has a much better plan: Never birthday alone! "The fall I turned 50 and a good friend turned 40, we had a 90th birthday party! She told everyone I was really 55 and I, of course, told everyone she was really 45!"

Marla remembers when "my brother bought forty red roses and passed them out to forty of his wife's friends and family. They were told to drop by at forty different assigned times to give her their rose. Each person pretended they knew nothing of the other thirty-nine roses. It went on from 7:00 A.M. until midnight. She loved it!" What fun to be one of the rose-delivering friends, too.

The Good News Is . . .

Friends may know how to "push your buttons" by the time you're 40, but they also know how to soothe your hurts and help you get back on your feet. Imagine being part of a Bunco club which has had the same members and meeting date for the past twenty-nine years:

We started as young brides, newly married, thin, full of hopes and dreams, and seeing life through rose-colored glasses. As the years have passed, our rose-colored glasses have turned into prescription bifocals. The brides and grooms in our lives are now our children, and we still have hopes and dreams of being able to sleep all night and not hear a door open or telephone ring. We have learned about clothes that shrink in the closet, and how signs have become smaller.

When we share our pictures of grandchildren, we also have to share our glasses. We've also given up on playing Bunco—we couldn't keep track of the dice and the conversation at the same time—and have what we jokingly call our group therapy sessions. Does it save us money! I have learned that no matter how successful one is or how much money one makes, life would be very empty without our friends.

Patricia, 48

The day dawned innocently enough. I had the usual "razzing" from my family, but nothing I couldn't handle. By 10:00 A.M., all that changed. I had just backed out of my driveway when I noticed a neon sign at the end of my street announcing my big day. In fact, there were signs all along the route to my job—my friends had borrowed real estate signs, covered them with neon poster board and wrote on them in big letters. In a town of fifty thousand, all but four people knew that I was turning 40 before the day was over. Six months later when I went in to get my dental checkup, the dental assistant told me she had seen my signs, and my mail carrier shared with me how everyone in the local post office was talking about it when they returned to the main post office that afternoon!

Pam from Oklahoma, 40

REASON 33

You can toss
out the alarm
clock—your
hormones are
doing wake-up
calls.

YOU CAN TOSS OUT THE ALARM CLOCK—YOUR HORMONES ARE DOING WAKE-UP CALLS.

When it comes to hormonal changes, there are lots of myth-conceptions:

1. A typical hot flash will last three to six minutes.
False!
By the time you dry your hair and put your makeup back on, we're talking twenty minutes, minimum.

2. Men will not understand what you are going through.
False!
Around 900 B.C., King David wrote, "My heart was hot within me; / While I was musing, the fire burned."[19] Sounds hot-flashy to me!

3. You will experience emotional and physical changes that may be unfamiliar to you.
False!
Symptoms of hormonal upheavals include: Irritability, lethargy, depression, headaches, forgetfulness, weight gain, insomnia, joint pain, backache, palpitations, crying spells, constipation, and decreased libido, *which are identical to the symptoms of PREGNANCY!* So don't tell us this is "something new." We're traveling recognizable territory indeed.

Jewel from Oklahoma defines 40-something as "too young for Social Security and just right for hot flashes." Linda, 47, bemoans the challenge of "not knowing when the 'power surges' are going to hit!" Sally, 46, says, "Hot flashes aren't much fun, but interesting." Keep humming that old standard (with a new twist), "I've Got My *Flashes* to Keep Me Warm."

Every woman has her own solution. Elaine from Washington admits, "You find yourself stepping out onto the porch at all hours of the day and night, enjoying the breeze, or opening the refrigerator and just standing there basking in all that cool air and secretly hoping it will activate some estrogen hiding somewhere in your body."

Of course, sleeping through the night may have become a fond memory of days gone by. "This was my situation: The heat consumed me in the daytime and the cold at night, and sleep fled from my eyes."[20] Sound familiar? Some mornings I sit up in bed at 4:00 A.M., suddenly wide-awake. The rest of the house is snoring away while I tiptoe around looking for something to read to help me nod back out. I'm going through about four novels a week.

Those early morning wake-up calls mean that I fold up like a card table at nine o'clock at night. The woman who could easily go until midnight is suddenly ready for beddy-bye not long after I tuck in the kids. I must not be the only one, because the eleven o'clock news is being replaced by the ten o'clock news. They're even backing up the six o'clock news to "Alive at Five!" because they're more certain we will be. I can see the day on the horizon when catching the news at noon will be my best option if I hope to stay awake all the way through to the weather.

Linda, 48, sees a plus here: "I get very prompt service at the deli counter. They must think I'm going to fall asleep if I have to stand in one place too long!"

Here's another plus: According to statistics, you need an hour less of sleep than you did at 20. Now that my bedtime is, by necessity, much earlier, I play a trick to make myself stay awake when driving home from an evening presentation. I move the time on my dashboard clock back two or three hours as soon as I hit the road. I keep telling myself, "Hey, it's only nine o'clock!" when in fact it's after midnight. Works like a charm. I even saw a pillow in a gift catalog that celebrated this concept, embroidered with these wise words: "It's later than you think."

*One way to chill out when you're having a
private summer.*

We wore mood rings in the seventies, but mood *swings* are something else again. Elaine, 40, seems to be enjoying hers: "I wish someone would say something to me and make my day. After letting them have it, I could turn around and say, 'My goodness, my hormones must be out to lunch today. I would *never* say anything like that, normally!'"

A friend of mine with a cranky mother is certain that some hormones could improve her mother's disposition drastically. I wonder. Could you sneak an estrogen patch in her slip? Her socks? Her Isotoner gloves? Rita doesn't find patches very user-friendly:

> *Considering all the Band-Aids I've applied in 40 years, you'd think attaching an estrogen patch would be easy.*
>
> *Not! It got stuck on my underwear on the way up, then half folded into a wrinkled mess. After ten minutes of trying to smooth it out, I just put a Band-Aid over the patch to hold it in place and wore it for an entire week like that!*
>
> Rita, 45

It might take more than a Band-Aid to patch things up at Louise's house, where she and her son are "going through menopause and preadolescence at the same time. Two people with erratic, raging hormones in the same house at the same time is often very explosive. (He just informed me that he wanted to pierce his ear.) He keeps me young and keeps me laughing."

The Good News Is . . .

Laughter is the best way to handle all those moments when you'd rather scream. Crying works, too, or you might try all three at once for faster relief. "I grow nostalgic and wistful and sometimes teary. Could that be premenopausal hormones?" wonders Carolyn, 47. I concur: It's those tears that catch me off guard, and anything can set me off.

Bill panics. "What's the matter, Liz? Are you okay?"

"No!" I wail, snurfling as I grope for a tissue in my bag. (*Snurfling* is not a typo. Unlike sniffling, which is a little dainty sound, *snurfling* is a full-bodied kind of thing requiring immediate attention.) Women over 40 not only need tweezers in their purse, they need tissues as well.

Tears and laughter have this in common: They both provide an emotional release, burn calories, ruin your makeup, and leave you feeling much better. You can do these activities alone or wherever two or three are gathered, and both are easily explained away by flashing a smile and saying sweetly, "I have PMS—Premenopausal Stress. Back up, please."

REASON 34

Menopause
means you can
enjoy a little
"whine" with
dinner.

MENOPAUSE MEANS YOU CAN ENJOY A LITTLE "WHINE" WITH DINNER.

One morning a farmer made his usual rounds at the henhouse, and discovered one hen had laid a stack of pennies instead of eggs. He figured someone was playing a trick on him, slipped the coins in his pocket, and went about his business. The next morning, the same hen surprised him again: This time, a handful of nickels waited under her feathers. The next day, it was dimes, the following day, quarters! Exasperated, the farmer called the vet to ask him what could possibly be happening to his hen. "Not to worry," the vet told him. "She's just going through the change."

If the average age for menopause among American women is 51, you could go through your entire 40s without a single symptom. The rest of us will hate you for this, but you could do it. My doctor also assures me that about 15 percent of women will have no symptoms of "the change" ever, except for the welcome one—no more visits from your "friend" (and who came up with *that* euphemism?) Keep telling yourself, "Hey, I could be in the lucky 15 percent!" Prayers are also helpful here.

Since the average life expectancy for a woman is 80, though, we're still talking thirty years without estrogen. Stock up now. Brenda, 53, warns her younger sisters, "Forty was a piece of cake. Fifty and menopause is the challenge."

Opinions are varied. Buni thinks the Big M is "God's gift to women," setting us free from many concerns. On the other hand, "a black hole" is how Phyllis describes it, and Mary Lee thinks it's "the pits!" Since my older sisters live many states away from me, I missed watching them go through that valley called The

Change. I was a mere 7 when my mother moved into menopause, so I didn't pay much attention then either. I'm counting on you, my friends, to enlighten me:

> *For the last six months of my 40s I had the worst pity party of my life. I'd been a stay-at-home mom and my youngest was graduating from high school, so my "job" was done and I had no Plan B. I was doing menopause big time and nobody wanted to hear about it, plus I was reaching the half-century mark. Bad combination.*
>
> Kay, 51

Some of us are already good whiners at 40; imagine our level of expertise by the time we hit menopause! (By the way, why is it called *menoPAUSE*? Shouldn't it really be *menoSTOP*? Or *menoCEASE*? How about *menoHASTA LA VISTA, BABY*?) We've already discussed some of the symptoms of the hormonal hurricane season. Here are a few more.

> *I almost cringe answering this. If this comment reaches print, anyone who knows me will know I wrote this. How embarrassing! I guess I'd have to say the most challenging thing about life after 40 is the weakening of the bladder muscles. I love to laugh and so I'm learning to tolerate "dampness" with joviality! When I get tickled, I trickle!*
>
> Karen, 42

I don't know why *Karen from Indiana* was so worried about sharing this bit of truth with us—we *all* understand exactly what she's talking about. Marlene from Washington calls it her "I.B.B.—Itty-Bitty Bladder," which wakes her every four hours. A Michigan woman admitted that she watched a woman waving her underwear over the hand dryer in a public rest room and *not one woman present said a thing.* Of course not. We get it. We don't like it, but we get it.

One of my birthday cards captured the essence of post-40 whining: "Millions of people turn 40 every day, but do they pout and complain and snap at everyone? Sure they do, old people are like that!" Joni, 41, finds herself complaining about health difficulties: "Nothing fatal, but weird stuff that friends usually don't want to hear about but probably deal with themselves."

Why are we whining? Simple: It's our turn. As children, we listened to our grandparents moaning and groaning about their health. As teenagers, we put up with our parents mumbling and grumbling about money. As college students, we tolerated professors fussing and fretting over our term papers. As loyal employees, we endure bosses grieving and grousing about profits and losses.

Now it's our chance to serve some whine with dinner. Hope from Virginia offers a glassful: "Maybe the worst thing is the realization that life won't go on forever. And, less profoundly, that your stomach probably won't get smaller, and the aches and pains will continue to increase for no good reason."

Whine on, sister.

Joanna, 42, finds herself "fighting the 'been there, done that' approach to life." Or as author and friend Joyce Landorf Heatherly says, "Been There, Done That, Bought the T-shirt." I'm guilty as charged on this count, as I watch my impatience rise over little things like customer service bloopers—getting cut off on the phone, finding an overcharge on my grocery receipt, discovering the wrong item in my Wendy's bag. Big deal, Liz. Get over it.

In theory, you'd think more years of experience would teach me the folly of getting upset about this stuff. That's not what's happening at my house. How about yours? Joanna says, "It's a challenge to keep freshness a part of so many things I do." Maybe that's what my problem is. Because I've "seen this all before," I don't really look at the situation with new eyes.

Then again, maybe I've just become a state-of-the-art whiner. Goodness knows, someone has to set the standard. Sing with me now: "Whine on, whine on harvest moon."

The Good News Is . . .

Once you compare your expectations with your experiences, life after 40 may actually give you less to whine about than you originally thought. Sally, 46, confesses having to get past "my own perceptions and myths about growing older. I keep expecting it to be more difficult and depressing than it really is."

So, in our 39th year, we'll panic. In our 40th year, we'll whine for all we're worth. Then in our 41st year, as the pressure of turning 40 gives way to the joy of just being in our 40s, we can relax for a few years before our hormones give out completely and the Big 5-0 brings its own set of challenges.

Meanwhile, remember: Menopause takes its toll. Please have exact change.

When I got home that evening, my husband had a nice dinner prepared and the girls were really excited. After dinner, the lights were dimmed and in they came with a birthday cake with forty candles. One problem: They were the kind that you can't blow out no matter how hard you blow. My husband ran into the kitchen and had to pull each candle out and run it under the water. But this process took so long the kitchen filled with smoke, which meant the fire alarm went off!!! We both ran around opening windows and sliding glass doors, trying to clear the smoke, while two little girls (then 3 and 5 years old) screamed their heads off. To top it all off, we couldn't eat the cake: The frosting had crystallized.

Lena from California, 42

REASON
35

Construction
workers leave
you alone—
no more
bothersome
whistling.

CONSTRUCTION WORKERS LEAVE YOU ALONE—
NO MORE BOTHERSOME WHISTLING.

Reason 35 always gets a big laugh from the audience, not only because it's true, but because it's one of the hardest things to accept about life after the Big 4-0: "It just kills me to have a gorgeous hunk look *through* me as he's checking out the cute, young things!" moans Kaye from Texas. Martha, 45, still admits it's a "shocking revelation that *I'm* not one of the cute, young things, even though I still feel like one in my heart."

I still remember walking down Prince Street in Lancaster, Pennsylvania, a 20 year old in a micro-skirt, long legs in full strut, as construction workers and cabdrivers whistled their approval. *I hated it! I loved it!* That's the truth. We didn't really like it, but oh, the agony when the whistles stop. Now, if someone whistles at me on the street, it's one long blast to get my attention: "Hey lady, the belt of your raincoat is dragging!"

Thank you so much.

Flying home from Las Vegas recently, I was sitting quietly in my aisle seat with two empty spots next to me, when two incredible hunks—I mean *hunks*—strolled into the coach cabin. We're talking Fabio here, we're talking muscles on display, tight jeans, curly hair, tan skin, sparkling eyes, sly smiles—be still, my beating heart. Actually, it stopped beating altogether when it became very clear where they were going to sit: next to me.

Gulp!

I smiled warmly as I stood up to allow them to climb into their seats. I pulled in my stomach and freshened my lipstick while they were looking out the window. I tried not to stare at those bronzed shoulders rubbing against mine as I struggled for some way to draw them into conversation. Everything I thought of sounded inane: "Do you two always look this good? Are you bodybuilders or just born hunks? Care to try lifting me, just for a lark?"

Taking a deep breath, I finally turned to the cutie in the middle, only to find out they had both *fallen asleep.* Dead to the world, snoring and drooling. So much for my ability to drive men to distraction with my charm and appeal.

Granted, there are some women over 40, over 50, who still hear whistling. Tina Turner has legs that will always stop traffic, and Jane Fonda still does a lot for a leotard. But for the rest of us, it's time to accept the fact that a handsome young man will probably find somewhere else to feast his eyes. As Carolyn, 48, wisely phrased it, "People start turning to you for your wisdom rather than your locks."

Come to think of it, what a blessing! My wisdom is always ready for action, while my looks take much longer to prepare for public viewing. As a matter of fact, when the two hunks on the plane woke up, they turned to *me* for directions to Baggage Claim, rather than asking the pretty young things across the aisle.

A certain freedom arrives with the realization that younger men aren't looking at you as a "hot mama" anymore, but rather as, well, a mama. Or a grandmama. Priscilla sees it as a big plus: "You don't have to check out the competition (you can't compete anymore), so now you can flirt with guys in their 20s. It's obvious that you aren't in the running and both of you are comfortable with it." Mary from Michigan affirms that "age gives you the courage to talk to anyone; you're too old to be considered a flirt."

So true! When I was 19 and worked as a bank teller, the management trainee in our department was certifiably gorgeous, a Don Johnson look-alike, who made my knees turn to jelly. The other women in our department, happily married and over 40, got along with him famously, teased him unmercifully, and flirted shamelessly. I couldn't put two words together because we were both single and I felt "looked over," and looked over. Major angst.

Now, when I have the opportunity to do business with junior hunks, I feel zero pressure to measure up—are you kidding?—and I just enjoy them as people. They seem to have fun with the banter as well, since they must grow weary of having to constantly compete with other guys to catch a beauty's eye. With an over-40 woman, they have our undivided attention. As Colleen McCullough, author of *The Thorn Birds*, put it, "The lovely thing about being 40 is that you can appreciate 25-year-old men more."

This Minnesota woman offers another angle on the appeal of younger men:

> *I recently started a new job and began flirting with a guy I only see at odd occasions or in the lunchroom. One night we were talking about a group of us getting together after work, and this guy said he had to get home to help celebrate his mom's 40th birthday! Just knowing I was seven years older than his mother made me forget every word of conversation beyond that point.*

Patt, 47

The Good News Is . . .

The story doesn't always end that way: Sometimes May and September get together for a very warm romance indeed:

> *I was a single parent when I joined a singles Sunday school class and met the best-looking redhead I'd ever seen. When we got to know each other I found out he was thirteen years younger than I, even though it didn't seem like it. The age difference didn't bother us, so we started dating. Sensing that God had brought us together, we knew it "was meant to be." We married in 1989 when I was 41 and he was 28. One night we were out for dinner, ran into a couple whom we knew from playing softball, and discovered that he was twelve years older than his wife. My husband said, "Really? There's thirteen years' difference between Brenda and myself." Our friend just stared at him and said, "I didn't know you were that much older than her!" (Oops.)*

Richard and I still laugh about that to this day. We've never seen the age difference and neither has anyone else!

Brenda, 47

REASON 36

Bifocals let you look down your nose at everybody.

BIFOCALS LET YOU LOOK DOWN YOUR NOSE AT EVERYBODY.

The brochure at my optometrist's office made it all sound so simple: "If you're over 40 and are having trouble reading up close, you probably have a common and natural condition called *presbyopia*." Sounds more like the fear of becoming a Presbyterian.

Maybe decreasing vision *is* a spiritual problem: "Now the eyes of Israel were dim with age, so that he could not see."[21] Yes, Israel, we understand. So sorry bifocals weren't invented yet. They might have been a big help to you. *Might* is the key word here.

I'm embarrassed to admit this, but after everything I've shared with you among these pages, why hold back now? On the day that bifocals showed up at my life's doorstep, my eye doctor, a pretty 30-something redhead with flawless skin and perfect vision, leaned over, patted my hand (making me feel 4 or 74, I'm not sure which) and said softly, "It's time, Liz."

I could feel the tears rising in my throat. Blinking and swallowing, I plastered my face with a big, brave smile. "Great!" I said, but didn't mean it.

"You'll learn to love bifocals," she said, and didn't mean that either.

It was awful.

I ordered the "Progressive Addition Lenses" (the kind without the line), which the brochure insisted would give me "a full range of uninterrupted vision, more like the natural vision of your youth!"

Golly, can't they do better than *that*? By the time I was 21, my eyes tested at 20/350. I want the natural vision of a young woman who can see herself in the mirror from across the sink, something I've never experienced as an adult.

Rita, 45, says with a sigh, "I'll yield to gray hair and a few extra pounds, but vanity hangs tough when it comes to giving up my contacts for a pair of bifocal specs." Deb, 47, was equally appalled. "I finally admitted I needed them when I couldn't read the hymnal when I held it in the usual position, and I couldn't fasten a brooch because I couldn't see the clasp. I've compensated by buying several pairs of 'vanity glasses,' to match my moods or outfits!" Meanwhile, at Bonnie's house, she and hubby are both wearing trifocals. When they sit and chat "our heads bob around like those little dogs on the dashboards of cars!"

"Love at first sight" takes on a whole new meaning after 40: Now I *love* when I can *see* something. Anything. I bought an oversized seventeen-inch computer monitor, and still sit with my chin tipped up, trying to focus the bottom half of my bifocals on the words that are swimming mere inches before me.

"These darn bifocals!" Brenda, 55, fumes. "I get more laughs from family and friends as I step up to imaginary stairs and reach much higher than I need to. That line across my glasses is a real challenge."

Plenty of us put off the inevitable as long as possible, but time catches up with us. Karen, 46, wishes she had "arms long enough to hold reading material. If only arms could stretch like the skin on your neck does at 40!" My speaker buddy Bryan Townsend from Alabama suggests putting your wristwatch on your ankle to get far enough away to read the dial.

Christina, 47, has given up on "trying to read the small print of a phone book or newspaper. I now carry magnifying glasses and have a full-page magnifying sheet nearby." I used to buy my grandmother those magnifying sheets for Christmas. Hope Santa can fit one in my own stocking this year.

If you're weary of having your eye doctor insinuate that bifocal time is approaching, take a tip from Ellen, 43: "Every year my doctor asks, 'Having any trouble reading up close?' as if he can't

You invent clever ways of getting your watch far enough away to read the dial.

wait for me to break down and say 'Yes!' Since he's a few years older than me, this year I said, 'No, how about you?'"

After tripping my way up and down steps for a few weeks, I went back to my optometrist and asked if contact lenses were out of the question. She smiled brightly and said. "Oh no, we'd be happy to fit you with some new lenses that match your bifocal prescription. We call these monovision lenses." Drop the first two letters and it's closer to the mark: NOvision.

One contact uses your close-up prescription, good for reading or threading a needle. The other contact is for long-distance viewing, like driving a car or seeing who that woman is your husband is talking to across the room. A great concept, in theory. The problem is, they want you to wear both contact lenses *at the same time*!

I asked my doctor, "How will this work?"

She said, "Relax. Your brain will adjust."

"Adjust to what?!" I shrieked. With bifocals I move my head up and down, up and down. With monovision contacts, I shift my head back and forth, back and forth. This is waaay too confusing for my over-40 brain.

There are certain reading materials that are especially confounding: phone books, Bibles, legal contracts with lots of fine print, and menus. Ruth insists, "I had to get glasses or take along a flashlight to every restaurant where the menus were being printed smaller and smaller."

The Good News Is . . .

If you can see well enough to read this page—even with trifocals tipped back and an arm extender—thank the Lord you can see at all. This Alabama woman had an experience that has taught her much about what it means to be able to clearly see what matters most:

Last summer I lost the vision in my right eye, with a
30 percent possibility of also losing my left eye vision. I

really wasn't discouraged. I just considered it too big for me to handle.

One particular friend commented, "I don't understand how God could have allowed this to happen to you." Searching for the words to help her understand, I said, "Think of it this way . . . I just see a little less of man so I can see a little more of God."

Sandra, 48

I once made the statement to my husband, "If you don't take me to Hawaii for my 40th birthday, I'll take myself." At my birthday party, he handed me a large manila envelope with lots of brochures on the Hawaiian Islands. "Gee, this is neat, when are we going?" was my reply. Much to my absolute shock the crowd shouted out, "*Today!*" I said, "But I'm not packed!" and my two best friends said, "Oh, yes you are! What you don't have you can buy in Honolulu." Within fifteen minutes we were on our way to the airport. My next question was, "Does Lois (a friend I hadn't seen in ten years) know we're coming?" "No, we'd better call her!" Lois was so excited after the phone call she couldn't work and had to take the afternoon off. I'll never forget my 40th!!!

Marie from California, 53

REASON 37

Cotton
underwear and
flannel
pajamas:
Comfort over
cute.

COTTON UNDERWEAR AND FLANNEL PAJAMAS:
COMFORT OVER CUTE.

Was I 29? Or was it 33, perhaps? One year of my life, one very particular day, I stopped wearing slinky bikini underwear and began buying "sensible" underwear: 100 percent cotton, all the way to the waist.

I've never looked back. Judging from the rejects I see on the deep discount table in the lingerie department, there are plenty of us who've abandoned those foolish fripperies—lace waistbands, pink rosette designs, French-cut legs, black spandex bikinis, peekaboo cutouts—in favor of pure white, industrial strength cotton from thigh top to waist. They seem warmer, safer, more dependable. The older cotton gets, the softer it gets, just like us. Maybe that's the appeal, mixed with some childhood memories and great marketing by the National Cotton Council.

When the Frederick's of Hollywood catalog arrives (honest, I don't ask for it, it just shows up), I laugh not only at the outrageous getups, but the fabrics and trimmings that you and I *know* would be uncomfortable to wear. All the scratchy lace and polyester straps and pinned-on bows. (You're right, of course. Those outfits aren't intended for sleeping in.)

The house dressing at Lizzie's? Flannel. Long sleeves, over the knees, high neck, red plaid cotton heaven. Bill will tell you the truth: He likes these pajamas better than the Frederick's kind, just because they are softer. I do, too, of course. When the weather gets nippy, I add socks. Can a scarf and gloves be far behind? Of course, when those night sweats really kick in, we may have to retire the flannel for a season.

Dorothy from Oklahoma loves being long past 40 so she can "do things I have always wanted to. Like wearing very bright flowered kneesocks. My grandchildren just shake their heads and say, 'Leave Grandma alone, She's getting old and just having fun. We think she's cute.'"

Now if only they could come up with a bra as comfortable as the cotton undershirts we wore as children. I remember the day I gave up one for the other as if it were yesterday, instead of 1966. Some mothers made a big deal out of buying this particular foundational garment for their daughters. Judy's mom presented it to her in a pretty pink box filled with fluffy tissue paper and a special card: "Now that you're growing up."

Mary Ann got a matching slip and panties with hers, in bright solid magenta. Mary Ann couldn't wear a white blouse for weeks.

Sharon and her mother went to the store together to pick hers out. It was a special "trainer" model, AA, no batteries included, but it definitely counted. She was "in."

I casually mentioned buying a bra to Mother one day, who promptly "tsk-tsked" and assured me, "When you really need one, we'll buy you one." A quick check in the mirror told me that the need level was low. *Flat* didn't even describe the situation. *Concave* was closer to the truth.

Secretly, I toyed with the idea of visiting Charlotte's Dress Shop on Main Street and buying one myself. *Oh, the adventure of it! I'd never been there alone. Could I pull it off? Would Mom find out?*

One afternoon on the way home from school, after yet another humiliating "no show" in the locker room, I sneaked up the concrete steps and through the door into Charlotte's. The bell above the door tinkled loudly. I licked my dry lips, eyes darting about, as I prepared to ask a clerk the dreaded question: "Where are your . . . foundations?"

Thank goodness, there they were on full display. Not like the nylons Mother bought me, which came in little flat boxes stacked floor to ceiling behind the counter. No, these mysterious wonders were each in their own box with a see-through window. Apparently, you simply picked one out, marched to the counter, plunked down your money. No problem!

Wait. Big problem. 32A? 34B? 36C? What in the world did those mean? I was an A– student. Did I need an A– bra? As I peered at the confusing array, I sensed someone moving toward me and spun around to find Charlotte herself, grinning knowingly, tape measure in hand.

"Were you looking for a particular size, dear?"

Gulp.

"Slip your jacket off and let's see what we need, shall we?"

We needed a 32. Actually, we needed a 28, but they didn't make those. She measured at the full part, too. Twenty-eight inches. (For the record, my waist was also a 28.)

She chose the most promising box from the top corner of the rack and pulled it out. An embarrassing blush started creeping up my neck and around my ears as she directed me toward the dressing room. In a minute, she would know the truth: I didn't need a bra at all.

I think she noticed, but didn't say a word except, "How does it feel?"

It felt like heaven. I smiled in the mirror, imagining my very own Playtex marvel making its debut at my next gym class. Never mind that the cups pooched out like empty pockets. I was finally going to be "in."

"I think this will do, don't you?" Charlotte purred, heading for the register. "That'll be $7.95 plus tax. Shall I charge it on your mother's account?"

"NO!" I almost shouted, then blinked back tears. *$7.95? I had no idea!* "No thanks, I'll just, uh, come back for it tomorrow."

Undershirts were $2.50, tops. I had $4.00 to my name. Who could have imagined such an exorbitant price for something so small? I dragged myself home, more discouraged than ever. No way was I bringing this up with Mom again. I would have to find another solution.

That solution was waiting for me in the trash can. My sister Mary, nine years my senior, had tossed out an old bra that had lost its zip. No question, it would take some effort to turn a 34B into a 28AAA, but I was desperate. Firing up our Singer sewing machine, I stitched the cups as flat as I could make them, added new seams to each side, and adjusted the shoulder straps.

Ta-da! It looked awful and felt worse, but if I moved fast in the locker room, no one would notice. I washed it by hand so Mother would never be the wiser and hid it in my closet to dry.

The next day in gym class, my pathetic excuse for a bra was nonetheless greeted with junior high enthusiasm—they even wrote a cheer to celebrate, along the lines of "Give me a B! Give me an R! Give me an A!" I was delirious.

Got away with it, too, for nearly a week, until I carelessly tossed my makeshift bra into the laundry hamper Friday afternoon. By the time I remembered, Mom had gathered up the clothes and headed for the laundry room. I was toast for certain.

Mom never said a word. Not Saturday, not Sunday. I was in agony all weekend. Monday morning, I found a plain white box on the top of the laundry basket. *Yikes! Mary's recycled bra with a stern note?*

I lifted the lid, grateful no one was watching my hands as they shook. "Oh my!" I said aloud, my spirits lifting instantly. It was a brand-new, lace-trimmed, ribbon-sporting brassiere, better than anything Charlotte's had to offer. Perfect for a young lady in training.

A voice from the doorway brought up my head with a snap. "I realized it was time," Mom said, smiling slightly, watching me with something like regret in her eyes. "Welcome to womanhood, Honey."

I didn't trust myself to speak, so instead I pressed my cheek against hers and squeezed my eyes tight enough to hold back the tears. Finally I managed to whisper, "Thanks, Mom."

My mother almost never laughed out loud. She laughed out loud.

"Don't thank me for *that*, daughter dear! You'll be anxious to get rid of them soon enough, believe me."

As usual, Mom was right.

The Good News Is . . .

I have it on good authority that, by popular demand, they are working on a flannel brassiere, in red plaid or traditional gray. Stretch straps. Stretch back. No seams. No wires.

Watch your mailbox.

REASON
38

No more jokes
about being
Jack Benny's
age.

NO MORE JOKES ABOUT BEING JACK BENNY'S AGE.

Karri from Utah was 39 when she completed her survey for this book. Well, at least that's what she wrote down: "My husband says that the year you're 39, you may as well be 40 for two years because no one believes you anyway!" Julie from Michigan couldn't agree more: "Friends say, 'Yeah, I've been 39 fifteen times. How many is this for you?' I was so glad to turn 40."

No doubt about it, the Jack Benny jokes get old (and just for the record, no matter what Benjamin Kubelsky told us, he lived for forty years *times two*—81 years, all of them as memorable as he was). Jewel from Oklahoma is past the age Jack Benny was when he left this earth; she, too, has tried to remain 39 forever:

All my life I heard comments about "old women" who probably were 40 years old, so I decided early in life not to turn 40. Each birthday after I reached 39, my family would just say, "Oh, Mama is 39 again." When my oldest daughter reached 39, she refused to say that we were twins, so I finally had to start increasing my age. But I avoided turning 40 for nineteen years!

Gail from California has another clever way of handling the "How old are you?" question. She confesses, "I am not a good 'untruth' teller. So all through my 40th year I had to admit, 'I'm 40.' Believe it or not, I was actually glad to hit 41 because from that point on I could honestly say, 'I'm not quite 40!' (This can be said for many years!)"

My friend Luan, 48, admits that she has fibbed about her age for so long that when she finally fessed up and started telling people the truth, she was accused of lying! Mary, 43, came up with a concept we'll call "spiritual math," since she figures, "Counting

my age from the date of my baptism, I am only 35." Good thinking, Mary. Bad math, but good thinking.

Bill often refers to someone as being "of indeterminate age."
Actually, that's most of us. I'm seldom correct when I guess a person's age beyond 10. With little ones, you can tell by motor and
language skills, but once we're all walking and talking, it's a
tough call. I wouldn't dare guess out loud because you never
know when you're going to step on someone's toes.

I recently served on the federal jury in Owensboro.
We had several flights of stairs to negotiate from the
courtroom and back to the jurors' room in the base-
ment. After one session we were descending the stairs
and one young lady, probably in her 20s, said, "My
knee hurts. I feel just like some old woman about 45!" I
said, "Yeah, I know what you mean!"

June, 48

True confession time: I'm not as tolerant of younger women as I should be. After all, I expect a 60-year-old woman to understand what I'm dealing with, so why shouldn't I be every bit as compassionate toward a 22-year-old woman who breaks her nail? (Sorry. There I go again.) As Janie, 56, sees it, "People 30–35 look incredibly childlike." We are not alone in our thinking:

When I see a young (20-ish) woman—the kind who doesn't have to suck in her tummy and doesn't have any bags under her eyes—I think to myself as I hear her start speaking, "Girl, have you got a lot to learn!" Then I wonder how old she will be when her brain finally starts to develop.

Jill, 48

Okay, okay. We'll stop here. If you've never had such feelings toward younger women, you are a *much* better person than I am! Sandra, 47, is also trying to let go of her false assumption that "everybody younger than us is inexperienced or stupid." Such thinking does have a way of turning around and biting you when you least expect it.

My father, who is 74, recently got out of the hospital and my husband and I stopped by his house to check on him. We parked in front of the house and walked across the yard. By the time we came in the door, my mother was doubled over with laughter and Daddy had a rather contrite look on his face. Mom explained that when they were looking out the window, she said, "I wonder who that is?" and Daddy responded, "Oh that's some old woman and Bill." He was quite surprised that the "old woman" was me!

Deanna, 44

Whether your family and friends see you as too young to know anything or too old to be called young anymore, try not to let them ruin the turning point that 39 deserves to be. Marian, 45, remembers, "When I turned 39, I was told by a friend, 'This is the last good day of the last good year of your life!' I can honestly say, she was wrong!" It really does get better after 39. Vanessa, 44, declares, "Birthdays since 40 are fun! It means I made it another year, and God hasn't taken me home yet!"

The Good News Is . . .

Your age is only a number, the sum of all the years you've had to learn something about life so far. Wear the mantle of your age lightly, because tomorrow you will trade it in for another age, one day older. Choose any number you like to share with the public, as long as you know in your heart you still have much to learn.

Martha from Illinois says, "I entered my 30th year kicking and screaming. I felt that life was over, and there was nothing left to do. How dumb I was at 30! By 40, I'd discovered that age has nothing to do with it. Being old, middle aged, or young is a state of mind."

I decided to leave the country rather than turn 40—literally. I flew to Israel with two of my closest friends, so with the time zone changes, I got to celebrate an extra six hours! I awoke to hotel mirrors covered with "40," birthday cards, and a Twinkie from home. I was serenaded with "Happy Birthday" on the tour bus on the way to the Old City, and spent the day seeing the Wailing Wall, the Temple Mount, Golgotha, and walking where Jesus walked. There were presents and faxes from home, from my kids, and one from work that everybody signed—a two-pager! That evening I shopped on Ben Yahuda Street and bought a gold cross to celebrate my faith. It was the best birthday I ever had!

Cherie from Ohio, 40

REASON 39

"Looking too young" never even crosses your mind.

"LOOKING TOO YOUNG" NEVER EVEN CROSSES YOUR MIND.

Your age is like a fairy tale: Hard to believe, no matter how many times it has been told.

Ruth from Ohio

And to think that we used to worry about wearing our hair too short, or our skirts too short, or our eyelashes too short, and risk *looking too young*. We added length to all three and hoped against hope that we would look older.

It was the ultimate compliment from a lifeguard at the beach: "Are you two seniors?"

We would bat our Mabelline-elongated lashes and giggle. "Seniors? Us? We're only sophomores!" We were thrilled to our toes.

It isn't until midlife looms on the horizon that the fear of looking too young is quietly replaced with a fear of looking too old.

The ultimate denial isn't "forever 39." It's "forever young." Where did they come up with this, "She's 42 years young" stuff anyway? Let's be truthful and say, "She's lived 42 years to date." So be it. Not old, not young, just alive.

Another "you can't kid a kidder" statement about aging is this one: "You're only as old as you feel." Uh-oh. Some days I feel 73. Of course, some days I feel 26, until I look in the mirror and reality rears its ugly head. Donna, 48, says, "I try to look young a little longer, but the problem is keeping the kids quiet!"

How about this definition of *old* from Terry, 45: "Old is always fifteen years older than I am." Talk about your moving target. "I've decided to put braces on my dentures so I look younger," says Ruth. She's 64. (As the Beatles would say, "Will you still need me? Will you still please me? When I'm . . .")

Younger people (that is, anyone who is pre-40) give us a run for our money. Sharon, 49, is struggling "trying to keep up with the younger folks at work! About four o'clock every day I'm finished. My brain has parked!"

Really young people (that is, those under 10) are especially helpful. Sandy from Nevada is a teacher whose students assured her, "You can't be that old! If you were that old—you'd be dead!" Cindy's 6-year-old neighbor wished her a Happy Birthday, then whispered in her ear, "Does this mean you're in the 4's column now?" Diana, 46, is amused when younger people say, "Oh, you could be my mother!" Marjorie is less amused when "young children look at you and you know they expect you to fall apart any minute." Merrigay says, "My 12-year-old daughter has recently nicknamed me 'Myrtle from the retirement home,' convinced I must be thinking, *That Walter Cronkite, he's a looker!*"

Never mind how kids see us, how do we see ourselves? I know the image I carry around in my head is the "Liz at 39" version, because that's literally what I'm working with: a set of publicity photos taken three years ago when I was 39. Between the advancing years and the receding hairline and the red instead of blonde, it's time for new photos, but 39 was such a good year! Look how long Ann Landers used *her* publicity photo. I promise I'll do a new set soon. Maybe next year. Maybe in the new millennium.

Linda from Alaska has got my number: "Most of us continue to view ourselves as remaining youthful while everyone our age is growing old before our eyes. Consider the typical class reunion." Ben remembers at his 60th birthday party, "all these senior citizens showed up talking incessantly about the weather, their medications, and their last BM. They claimed to be my classmates! Very unsettling. I told them I had a date, took the cake, and left."

Here's another tiny fib we tell ourselves: "Well, I'm young at heart." Good for you, but that part doesn't show. How about the rest of you? Pamela, 45, says, "I still think I'm in my 30s. When people are discussing the elderly they look at me and I glance over my shoulder to see who they're looking at (it couldn't possibly be me)!"

I wish I had a dollar for every time someone said to me, "When you get to 50, you need to write a book about 'Fifty Reasons Why Life Is More Fun After the Big 5-0'!" My editor will be the first to tell you, if I'd dawdled much longer on this one, that's what the title might have turned out to be! It's a whole new ball game at 50, for sure. Victor Hugo observed: "Forty is the old age of youth; fifty is the youth of old age." And as Phyllis puts it, "it only takes a few months for that ten years to pass by!"

The Good News Is . . .

Change is merely an opportunity for humor. Betty from Missouri believes that one sure sign that we're getting older is the changes in our language:

> *I was teaching a Sunday school lesson about the loaves and fishes, and explained to this group of junior high students that the loaves at that time would have been "what we think of as buns today." Needless to say the titters of the group made me aware of what I'd gotten myself into here!*

I too remember when *buns* were what held your hamburger together. Ah, the good old days, presently being traded in for the good *new* days!

REASON 40

It's the perfect time for looking inward, outward, forward, and upward!

IT'S THE PERFECT TIME FOR LOOKING INWARD, OUTWARD, FORWARD, AND UPWARD!

The great thing about getting older is that you don't lose all the other ages that you've been.

Madeleine L'Engle

It was Saturday night at a women's retreat in Michigan: Several hundred of us were having some serious fun, singing praise songs and listening to a woman named Robin play the piano. I'd spoken to the group earlier that day. Now it was my turn to relax and be taught.

Robin played classical music with such passion that night that it brought tears to our eyes. The grand piano was practically lifting off the stage when her hands hit the keyboard for the final chords. *Bong! Bong! Ba-bong!* We were breathless as we applauded wildly.

But Robin was not done.

Next she moved into a soft hymn that made us weep with a vision of all that is holy. The last chord echoed with gentle clarity and we blinked away silent tears, an image of the throne of heaven elegantly etched in our minds.

But Robin had more up her sleeve.

Her hands began to dance across the black-and-whites, her ample bottom began to dance across the padded bench, and our hearts began to dance in our rib cages as this holy woman, this former nun, started playing sanctified *boogie-woogie* with a righteous rhythm!

We were standing by this point. We were moving. Swaying. Before the night was over, we'd learned not only how to worship with all our hearts, but with our feet, too, and in the bargain, had learned the Macarena!

Robin is 55, but don't you believe it. In her heart, she is a child again, set free with the discovery that only when you give *all* of who you are to the One you love—every gift, every flaw, every facet of your personality—only then are you free to experience Real Joy.

She radiated Real Joy that night. We had Real Joy just by being there. When I spoke the next morning, I threw out my notes (trust me, this is *not* my usual style!) and spoke from the heart about the healing power of laughter and the freeing power of giving everything to God and letting go of the outcome. I have never had more fun on the platform, and have never seen an audience laugh harder. Why? Robin showed us all how to let go and let God.

I stumbled upon a big "A-ha!" that weekend. For the first time in my 42 years, instead of looking at younger women and wishing I had their carefree attitudes and thin thighs, I found myself watching an older woman, wishing I could be more like her. Yes! This is real joy, knowing that "To everything there is a season, / A time for every purpose under heaven."[22] This is our season to be women over 40. Let's not waste a minute wishing it were otherwise. There's too much dancing and too much laughing to be done.

Jean from Delaware celebrates the delight of "finding your identity after years of searching—and liking what you find!" Sally from Ohio confesses, "I am smarter and sexier and more comfortable in my own skin than I've ever been." Mary Ann from Georgia reminds us, "You can't turn back the clock but you can wind it up again."

And I love Maria's enthusiasm: "I've finally grown up! Can you imagine spending thirty-nine years growing up? It's only been fun since 40! How come it took so long!?" Mickie sounds like she's been set free, too: "As I grow older, I find that what I have to say or do is no sillier than anyone else!"

A woman turning 40 can be an energy force turned loose. June-Carolyn from California says her life had become "so routine it was dull. I felt I was existing, not living. Then a spark ignited inside me. I drove straight to the local college and enrolled in two classes, even though I hadn't been in school for twenty years." As Terry points out, "All this talk about being over the hill fails to take advantage of the view from the top."

From your 40th birthday celebration forward, you need to decide that this decade is a gift to be opened and enjoyed. Paula admits, "surrounded by my friends and family, the 40th birthday I fought so hard against was a real celebration." Vanessa, 44, urges us to "wisely use what time we have, and the wisdom we've accumulated, to make the most of our lives."

Lois from Montana is looking at life after 40 with a new view:

So many things have changed this year. I was diagnosed with multiple sclerosis (bad); I've developed a new music career (good); I have more credibility in the community (good); I'm about to fall in love (very good!); and the MS hasn't quieted my voice (very, very good)!

The French novelist Colette declared, "What a wonderful life I've had! I only wish I'd realized it sooner." Now is a good time to realize it. Actually, any time is a good time. Are you 30? Begin. Approaching 40? Awareness awaits you. Ready for 50? Life is ready for you. Just short of 60? What are you waiting for? Soon 70? Say yes now! Almost 80? It's never too late to have a wonderful life.

Since I suspect that I'll be on to other projects when my 50th rolls around, and may have retired my computer by my 60th, and hope to be busy with grandchildren by my 70th, and may be in heaven before my 80th, then let's consider right now what those future "major decades" are going to hold for us

Fifty is fabulous, according to the women we heard from who called it "life-affirming," "a relief," and "like waking up." Judith, 53, shares: "Fifty was spent alone. I considered it a Rite of Passage. I had time to reflect on the past and look ahead with a plan and direction that I want to pursue. Every day is important, and yet I find reflection very comforting."

"Over the hill?"
You bet . . . and what a view!

Sixty looks super when seen through the eyes of a woman who has been there. Kay, 62, says you have "enough experiences under your belt to take life as it comes, with the assurance that in both the good and bad times, happy and sad times, God is there bringing meaning and purpose in all times."

Seventy sounds stupendous, according to Flo, 72, who remembers "My 70th birthday was my first birthday party in sixty-three years and by far the better of the two. (So few showed up at my 7th birthday, due to a more affluent party on the same day, same street!) On my 70th, all my friends came to a potluck party given by my youngest daughter. The entire theme was, "Aged to Perfection."

Eighty is awesome, at least when you're Elsie: "If you survive until you are 80, everybody is surprised that you're still alive. They treat you with respect for having lived so long. (Actually, they seem surprised that you can walk and talk sensibly!) People forgive you for everything. If you ask me, life begins at 80."

The Good News Is . . .

If Elsie is right, and life begins at 80, then why sweat 40? You're only halfway to the best part. (I am *not* suggesting you are a half-life. That's reserved for certain radioactive substances. You're lively, all right, but not deadly!)

This next story may seem contrived, but you'll just have to trust me, every word is true. As my brother Tom is fond of saying, "I kid you not!"

I rode on a hotel shuttle bus in Montana a few months ago with a woman who was delighted to tell me she was 80. "What brought you to Great Falls?" I asked her, just making conversation.

She'd spent a week at a dude ranch, that's what. That was after spending four days in Portland, Oregon, riding a big paddle wheeler up the Willamette River. Alone.

"What prompted you to do that?" I asked her, amazed.

"My friends just got back from there and said it was not to be missed," she explained. Apparently, this woman missed nothing.

"I already had a trip to California lined up, but managed to squeeze in Portland. I've been on the road for a month."

I am speechless. At 42, I can barely handle four days on the road.

She continued, "I just hope my ankle won't bother me."

I looked down to examine her bundled foot. "My! What happened?" I asked, genuinely concerned for this spry adventurer.

"Oh, I twisted it horseback riding yesterday." With that, she eased out the door of the shuttle and headed toward the terminal calling out to no one in particular, "Can you tell me where I might find Alaska Airlines?"

I've just met my hero, and I don't even know her name. Happy trails, beautiful woman.

If I'm traveling the world in my 80th year, how comforting to know that even then I won't be alone. "Even to your old age and gray hairs / I am he, I am he who will sustain you."[23]

It was Sunday, July 4, 1993, and I was a nauseated, depressed, fat 40 year old who was eight months pregnant! Not a pretty picture. My 15-year-old son had agreed to spend one week at a Young Life Camp without knowing a single person (a great feat), and now a week later he was walking through the door with my husband. When I asked my son if he had a good time, he beamed. "It was wonderful!" He hesitated and added, "Mom, I have something to tell you. I accepted the Lord as my Savior." It was so unexpected and yet I had prayed so hard for this child of mine. I sobbed with joy at the never-ending grace of our Lord. I hugged this six-foot, 15-year-old precious angel, giving thanks to the Lord for again answering in a miraculous way. I said with all honesty, "Son, this is the best birthday present I've ever received!"

Beverley from Kentucky, 41

The Really Good News Is . . .

Forty fun reasons, and forty "good newses" later, you might wonder if anything could be more joyful than all that.

Well, for some women among us, a 40th birthday brought unexpected blessings:

I'd dreaded my 40th birthday, and my best friend Laura and I would talk and rib each other about it. Laura died in an automobile accident when she was 38, so on my 40th birthday, I did not mind being 40. I was just glad I was here to enjoy it, surrounded by a large loving family. I let them believe they had rubbed it in that I was now officially "old," but I was smiling inside, thankful for the happy life God has given me.

Doris, 44

An awareness of our own mortality and the fragile nature of life makes any birthday—any day—worth celebrating. When we reach 40, we not only look at the changes in our bodies and our emotions, we examine the changes in our spiritual selves, that part of us that reaches out to know and be known by the One who made us and loves us.

Christine, 43, finds herself "more spiritually settled—most of the time, not always!" Flo calls the 40s "Revival time!" and Terie, 39, sees the big leap to 40 as "one year closer to eternity."

My own discussions with God fall along these lines:

> Liz: *"Oh, Lord, what would I do without You?"*
> God: *"Not much."*

The most popular response on my "turning 40" survey was "It beats the alternative!" Depends on what you think the alternative is. If you think life as we know it is all there is, and death is the exclamation point that says, "The End!" then this life, however miserable, does beat *that* alternative.

But, if you believe in life after death, rather than death after life, then this earthly journey is just the part where we work things out with our Creator and Savior, knowing that His grace alone will carry us to glory. "Therefore we do not lose heart. Even though our outward man is perishing, yet the inward man is being renewed day by day."[24] In which case, however good this life is, the alternative can't possibly be beat!

I love the baseball cap that Carolyn from Georgia sent me for my 40th. It was black (of course) and said, "Forty Isn't Old—Eternally Speaking." So true! For your 40th year and beyond, I wish you buckets of Real Joy, tons of heartfelt laughter, gallons of tears that cleanse the soul, and the peace that comes from knowing God.

Carolyn, 47, offers the best benediction of all:

> *The best thing about being over 40 is that I'm a lot*
> *more mature in my faith now than I was in my younger*
> *years. Even though God isn't through with me yet, I feel*
> *that I know Him better now. Each day I'm one step*
> *closer to heaven and seeing Him face-to-face. That's the*
> *very best part of being over 40!*

Amen, sister! I hope to see *you* there, too. God bless and *Happy Birthdays* . . . from 40 to eternity!

Notes

1. Ps. 16:6
2. Gen. 18:12
3. Luke 6:21
4. Song 4:4
5. Acts 27:34
6. Matt. 10:30
7. Est. 6:1 NIV
8. Deut. 8:4
9. Job 18:9 NIV
10. Prov. 16:31
11. 1 Cor. 11:15
12. Eccl. 3:15
13. Prov. 5:18
14. Jer. 4:22
15. Prov. 23:5 NIV
16. Prov. 23:22 NIV
17. 2 Peter 1:13 NIV
18. Eccl. 4:10 NIV
19. Ps. 39:3
20. Gen. 31:40 NIV
21. Gen. 48:10
22. Eccl. 3:1
23. Isa. 46:4 NIV
24. 2 Cor. 4:16

About the Author

Liz Curtis Higgs loves helping women laugh—on the air, in person, and in print. She entertained listeners on the radio for a decade (including singing "Happy Birthday" each day to some poor unsuspecting soul!). Then in 1986, Liz shifted her focus to the platform and now speaks to an average of fifty thousand women each year at conferences and retreats all over America. She's a columnist for *Today's Christian Woman* magazine and the author of seven books with Thomas Nelson Publishers, including *"One Size Fits All" and Other Fables* and *Only Angels Can Wing It, the Rest of Us Have to Practice.*

Her best source of material—and favorite audience—is her family: Matthew, 9, Lillian, 8, and hubby, Bill Higgs, who has a Ph.D. in Old Testament Languages and serves as director of operations for her speaking and writing business. Bill and Liz produce a fun, informative newsletter, *The Laughing Heart®*, mailed twice yearly *FREE* to more than twelve thousand readers around the world. For your free copy of her newsletter, or for any other information about her presentations and products, please write:

Liz Curtis Higgs
P.O. Box 43577
Louisville, KY 40253-0577

Give yourself more reasons to smile with other books from Liz Curtis Higgs . . .

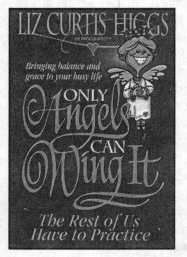

Only Angels Can Wing It!

One of the funniest, most encouraging women around, Liz Curtis Higgs reexamines the many qualities of the "virtuous woman" taking the pressure off today's well-meaning but weary (and less than angelic) wives and mothers. Liz addresses everything from fiscal responsibility to maintaining a happy, comfortable home without burning out. . . showing women we're doing better than we thought.

0-7852-8247-5 • Trade Paperback • 228 pages

Reflecting His Image

Humorist and author Liz Curtis Higgs offers an alphabetical journey through God's Word, as she weaves together twin themes that lead to the biblical view of self-worth: Who Christ is in you and Who you are in Christ.

0-8407-6335-2 • Hardcover • 128 pages
0-7852-7109-0 • Printed Casewrap • 128 pages